Dr. G

How to Be a People Helper

You Can Help The Others In Your Life

Regal Books
A Division of Gospel Light
Ventura, California, U.S.A.

Published by Regal Books
A Division of GL Publications
Ventura, California 93006
Printed in U.S.A.

Except where otherwise indicated, all Scripture quotations in this book are taken from the *New American Standard Bible*, Copyright © The Lockman Foundation 1960, 1962, 1963, 1968, 1971, 1972, 1973, 1975. Used by permission.

HOW TO BE A PEOPLE HELPER
Copyright © 1976 by Vision House/Regal Books
All rights reserved

Library of Congress Catalog Card Number 76-15112
ISBN 0-8307-1346-8

18 19 20 21 22 23 24 25 / 93 92 91 90

Rights for publishing this book in other languages are contracted by Gospel Literature International (GLINT) foundation. GLINT also provides technical help for the adaptation, translation, and publishing of Bible study resources and books in scores of languages worldwide. For further information, contact GLINT, Post Office Box 488, Rosemead, California, 91770, U.S.A., or the publisher.

As with any skill, people helping improves with practice.

Discover how you can develop your people helping skills and help those you love and care about deeply.

ACKNOWLEDGMENTS

The author gratefully acknowledges the cooperation of the following publishers, who have given permission to quote from the sources listed below:

Abingdon Press—For excerpts from Howard J. Clinebell, Jr., *Basic Types of Pastoral Counseling*, copyright 1966, and *Mental Health Through Christian Community*, copyright 1965.

Charles C. Thomas—For excerpts from D. Lester and G.W. Brockopp, *Crisis Intervention and Counseling by Telephone*, copyright 1973.

Christianity Today—For excerpts from J.W. Drane, "Fellowship: Our Humpty-Dumpty Approach," copyright 1975.

Prentice-Hall—For excerpts from Albert Ellis and Robert A. Harper, *A Guide to Rational Living*, copyright 1961.

Public Affairs Committee—For excerpts from C.J. Frederick and C.J. and L. Lague, *Dealing with the Crisis of Suicide*, copyright 1972.

Regal Books—For excerpts from Ray C. Stedman, *Body Life*, copyright 1972.

Tyndale House—For excerpts from Paul Morris, *Love Therapy*, copyright 1974.

Van Nostrand Reinhold—For excerpts from S. Jourard, *The Transparent Self* (rev. ed.), copyright 1971 (by Litton Educational Publishing, Inc.).

Victor Books—For excerpts from W.A. Hendrichsen, *Disciples Are Made—Not Born*, copyright 1974.

Word Books—For excerpts from Keith Miller, *The Taste of New Wine*, copyright 1965.

Zondervan Publishing House—For excerpts from J. Dwight Pentecost, *Design for Discipleship*, copyright 1971.

To

PAUL TOURNIER,

my friend

and mentor,

who showed me

how to really be

a people helper.

CONTENTS

Be sure to use the abilities
God has given you. . . .
Keep a close watch on all you
do and think.
Stay true to what is right
and God will bless you
and use you to help others.

1 Timothy 4:14, 16, *The Living Bible*

PREFACE

Helping people with their problems is everybody's business. Psychologists, psychiatrists, social workers, and other professionals have special expertise in this area, but in one way or another all of us are involved in counseling, perhaps almost every day. Guiding our children through a crisis, counseling a bereaved neighbor in her grief, advising a teenager about his dating behavior, listening to a relative describe the problems with a wayward or retarded son, encouraging the family of an alcoholic, helping one's mate to cope with a difficult work situation, guiding a young Christian through a period of doubt—all of these are counseling situations, whether we realize it or not. And most of these situations are handled effectively by laymen, whether they feel qualified or not. Even if there were a sufficient number of professional and pastoral counselors to handle everybody's needs, some people would still prefer to discuss their problems with a neighbor or friend. Friends are close by, they don't charge fees, and they are often easier to talk to than a stranger who goes by the awesome title of "counselor." Nonprofessional people helpers may have little or no training, but they nevertheless are making a significant impact and are on the front lines of the mental health movement.

Until now, little has been written to assist the Christian lay counselor (or *paraprofessional,* to use the term by which these people are usually described in psychological literature). Almost nothing exists in print to show that counseling can and must be a vital part of the church's outreach to rundown others. Several years ago we came to realize that evangelism was not a responsibility only for pastors and Billy

Graham. Books began to be written which showed that evangelism was the task of laymen who were trained by church leaders. Now the time has come for us to make the same shift in the area of counseling. The layman, especially the Christian layman, must take greater responsibility in meeting the needs of those who seek solace, friendship, or counsel. People helping is not something that we can leave solely to professionals or busy pastors.

It is the theme of this book that Christian counseling must be built on the Bible as the Word of God and must be consistent with the Great Commission, in which Jesus commanded His followers to make disciples of all nations. So relevant is the concept of discipleship to the act of people helping that we begin this book with a discussion of the important topic of discipleship. From this it does not follow that competent people helpers will disregard the techniques of psychology, psychiatry, or the other helping professions. Nor does it assume that we can learn to help people just by reading a book, that all of us will be equally effective, or that we will each counsel in exactly the same way. We are all individual personalities with unique gifts, mannerisms, and approaches to people. Such individuality need not be squelched, but it should be channeled in ways that will make each of us more effective as helpers and more sensitive to the leading of the Holy Spirit as we seek to assist others.

In the following pages we will take a look at counseling past and present, including professional and pastoral counseling as well as counseling by laymen. This is the major thrust of Part 2 of this book. The main purpose of this whole volume, however, is not to give a survey of a changing field or to add to the increasing number of books on counseling. Instead, our chief goal, as presented in Part 1, is to give practical guidelines for assisting Christians to effectively help relatives, friends, fellow churchmen, and others with their problems. There is no attempt to discredit the counseling professions or to suggest that highly trained counselors are unnecessary. I number myself among those who are called professional counselors and I respect the work of my colleagues. But I also realize (as do some of my colleagues) that many people are doing effective counseling, often with little or no training. This book is written to help them—to help you—do this task with greater skill and efficiency.

As with any skill, people helping improves with practice. There are ethical reasons which should keep us from practicing newly acquired counseling skills on people with real problems. It is suggested, therefore, that beginners learn in groups—encouraging and trying out their emerging skills on one another. A growthbook manual to facilitate this learning has been designed to accompany this book and has been tested in both church and educational settings. (The *People Helper Growthbook* is available from Vision House.)

Several years ago a government-sponsored study discovered that when people had personal problems only 28 percent of them went to professional counselors or clinics. Approximately 29 percent consulted their family physician and 42 percent sought help from clergymen. Little wonder that doctors are overworked and pastors are swamped with impossible caseloads—so much so that thousands of needy people are doing what they have done for centuries—turning to friends for advice and encouragement in times of need. The government study concluded that "a host of persons untrained or partially trained in mental health principles and practices—clergymen, family physicians, teachers . . . and others (including laymen)—are already trying to help and treat the mentally ill in the absence of professional resources. . . . With a moderate amount of training through short courses and consultation on the job, such persons can be fully equipped with an additional skill as mental health counselors." Theological education and other leadership training programs already are taking responsibility for training pastoral counselors. It is now time to help the layman do a better job. This is the responsibility of the counseling professions and the purpose of this book.

Many people, including my wife, Julie, have had an important impact on the development of this book, and I deeply appreciate their help. Larry Tornquist, Janet Poore, and

Georgette Sattler worked with me on the final preparation of the manuscript, and several of my students helped with the testing of the growthbook. Some of the material from Chapter 11 originally appeared in *Christianity Today,* and most of the remaining chapters were originally presented in lectures, seminars, and training sessions both at Trinity Evangelical Divinity School and at Conservative Baptist Seminary.

The people who interacted with the material in this book were people helpers to me. It is my sincere desire that the following pages will be helpful to you as you become a more skillful people helper.

—Gary R. Collins

The People Helper cassette tapes which cover all twelve of the study group sessions are available in a package produced by Vision House. The package includes the *How to Be a People Helper* book, the *People Helper Growthbook*, and three cassettes.

Part One

THE PRACTICE OF PEOPLE HELPING

1
PEOPLE HELPING AND THE GREAT COMMISSION

Shortly before leaving this earth and going back to heaven, Jesus gave His famous mandate to the little band of followers who had gathered together with Him on the mountain in Galilee. "Go and make disciples of all nations," He said, "baptizing them in the name of the Father and the Son and the Holy Spirit, teaching them to observe all that I have commanded you . . . ." Jesus assured the disciples of His power and of His presence "to the end of the age" (Matt. 28:18-20), and then He left them.

These men and women to whom Jesus spoke were already disciples. They had already decided to follow Jesus and to commit their lives fully to Him. They must have understood, at least partially, that because of divine love Christ had come into the world to die in place of sinful men. They must have recognized and confessed their sin and submitted completely to the risen Lord. It was to this dedicated group that Jesus gave a twofold responsibility. Discipling was to involve *witnessing* with the goal of winning people to Christ and *teaching* others what Jesus Himself had taught during His brief time on earth.

Jesus had taught that all men are sinners and in need of a savior. He had attacked the idea that a person is a child of God because of citizenship, parental beliefs, or good works. Instead, Jesus proclaimed that if any person wanted to have eternal life it was necessary to confess sin and yield his or her whole life to Christ's control. More important, Jesus taught that His death was to pay the penalty for the sins of mankind and make it possible for those who wanted to do so, to become children of God. The disciples were instructed to proclaim this message, to urge people to put their faith in Christ, to baptize these new believers, and to teach them from the Scriptures.

Someone has suggested that the Lord began His ministry by calling Peter, Andrew, James, and John to *become* disciples, that He ended His ministry with His Great Commission to *make* disciples, and that in between He taught people how to *be* disciples. In this process, Jesus approached people in a variety of ways. At different times He instructed, listened, preached, argued, encouraged, condemned, and demonstrated what it was like to be a true child of God. Perhaps no two persons were ever approached in exactly the same way, since Jesus recognized individual differences in personality, need, and level of understanding, and He treated people accordingly.

THE SCOPE OF THE GREAT COMMISSION

It does not appear that the Great Commission was limited to one geographical area or to one period of history. Neither is there any indication that the instructions of Jesus were limited to a few people, like pastors or other church leaders. Clearly Jesus intended all of His followers for generations to come to be involved in the business of making disciples—evangelizing and teaching new believers. Might it not be, therefore, that the Great Commission has relevance for people helping today? *Since being a disciple and making disciples is a requirement for all Christians, surely the discipling of others must be a part of Christian counseling—perhaps even its major goal.*

Before pursuing this controversial suggestion, it is important for us to think about the meaning of discipleship. In its broadest sense the word "disciple" means "student" or "learner." As used in the Scriptures, however, the term has a much stronger connotation. It implies the acceptance of the views and teachings of a leader to whom we are obedient. The people who enroll in my seminary classes are my students but they are not my disciples. They learn from me but they do not follow me in obedience and dedication. In contrast, Jesus came into the world not merely to teach students but to make disciples who would follow Him. He spent His life disciplining men and women. He ended His life on earth by commanding each of us to follow His example in making disciples (and by implication disciplers) of others.

THE CHARACTERISTICS OF DISCIPLESHIP

According to the Scriptures a disciple has at least three characteristics, is called upon to willingly pay three costs, and is given three responsibilities. As we will see, all of this is extremely important to people who call themselves Christians. It is of crucial significance to those who want to be Christian people helpers.

Obedience

Let us look first at the three characteristics of a disciple of Jesus Christ. The first of these is *obedience*. A disciple is a person who is committed to and obedient to the person and teachings of the Master. J. Dwight Pentecost has commented on this concisely:

> Christ demanded absolute submission to His authority, complete devotion to His Person, confidence in His Word, and trust in His provision, and men excused themselves because they would not commit, could not trust, and did not believe. . . . The disciples were those who, after they were convinced of the truth of the Word, completely committed themselves to the Person who had taught them. If one stops short of this total, complete commitment to the Person of Jesus Christ, he is not a disciple of Jesus Christ. He may be numbered among the curious, or he may even have progressed to the place where he is convinced of the truth of what Christ had to say or of what God's Word says, but until he completely commits himself to the Person whose Word he has come to believe, he is not a disciple in the full New Testament sense of the word. . . . One will not become a disciple simply because he assents to the truth of what Christ taught, but he becomes a disciple when he puts himself

under the authority of the Word of God and lets the Word of God control his life.[1]

According to Jesus' own teachings, we are truly His disciples when we abide in His Word (John 8:31). This would imply letting the Word of God exert absolute control over our lives and our obediently seeking to bring every aspect of life into conformity with Biblical teachings.

Love

The second characteristic of a disciple is *love*. "A new commandment I give to you, that you love one another, even as I have loved you," Jesus stated in John 13:34. "By this all men will know that you are My disciples, if you have love for one another." In a little booklet, Francis Schaeffer has called love the "mark of a Christian." It is the most obvious and unique characteristic of the disciple of Jesus Christ. And it is the most basic requirement for anyone who would seek to be a people helper.

When the Apostle John was writing his First Epistle, he realized that some of his readers were having difficulty knowing who were really Christians and who were not. To help with this problem John indicated that Christians were people who were characterized by love. If a person doesn't have love, John said, he probably isn't even a believer at all (1 John 4:7-11). Not all Christians are committed to being dedicated disciples of Jesus Christ, but all Christians have to be at least somewhat characterized by love. It is a contradiction in terms to think that one could be a true follower of Christ and not be loving.

Fruitfulness

The third characteristic of a disciple is *fruitfulness*. "By this is my Father glorified," Jesus stated, "that you bear much fruit and so prove to be my disciples" (John 15:8).

We live in a success-oriented society. Everybody wants

to be successful, and most of us are working on our various personal plans to reach this goal. In John 15, however, Jesus told His followers that all of these efforts would be useless unless the disciple was consistently committed to Christ, abiding in Him, and not trying to push ahead with his own schemes or relying on his own resources. Jesus used the example of grapevines which were not producing fruit. The best thing for them, He said, was that they should be broken off from the vine and burned in a fire.

Walter Henrichsen of the Navigators tells how he reacted when he first realized that God might come along someday and destroy man's self-centered work (2 Pet. 3:10). "What a shock . . . to realize that everything I planned to build, God would come along and destroy! I want you to know that discouraged me . . . . It was not worth it. Why give all my time and effort to build something which God had already said He will burn?"[2] So Mr. Henrichsen turned to the Bible and discovered that there were at least two things which God promised never to destroy: His Word (Isa. 40:8) and His people (John 5:28, 29). "There are other eternal things—God, angels, virtues such as love—but I wanted something enduring that I could grab hold of and give my life in exchange for. In setting my life's objectives I could give myself to *people* and *the Word of God* and know that God was not going to follow me and burn them up."[3]

THE COSTS OF DISCIPLESHIP

There are, however, some costs of discipleship. Bonhoeffer wrote a whole book about this,[4] and the Scriptures are very clear in stating that discipleship is not cheap. It is for this reason that nobody is ever recruited to be a disciple against his will. Some people are not willing to pay the cost. To be a disciple of Jesus Christ means that we must be willing to give up our closest relationships (Luke 14:25, 26), our personal ambitions (Luke 9:23), and our possessions (Luke 14:33).

Personal Relationships

Consider first our *personal relationships*. Jesus never tore down the family. On the contrary, He instructed us to respect our parents, love our mates, and teach our children, but the relationship that we have with Christ must take precedence over even the family. Some husbands and fathers have interpreted this to mean that they can leave their families to fend on their own while they go about "the Lord's work." Such an argument forgets that raising a family and fulfilling our obligations as family members *is* the Lord's work as much as pastoring a church, teaching in a seminary, or serving as a deacon. Surely God will hold us responsible for what we have done with the people in our families, but in terms of priorities we must be willing to put Christ first in our lives, even before our families.

Personal Ambitions

Perhaps it is even harder to lay aside our *personal ambitions*. In Luke 9, the 5000 people had just been fed and the disciples must have been feeling part of something very successful. It is then that Jesus announced that discipleship involves denying oneself (including one's personal ambitions), taking up a cross (the symbol of low status), and following Christ. Sometimes, of course, God does permit the disciple to attain a high status, and often he is able to reach his personal goals. But the disciple must be willing to give up his or her personal ambitions or have ambitions changed so that they conform to what Christ wants for our lives.

Very often we hear Christians talking about how they wanted something very badly, and when they committed their lives to the Lord they got exactly what they *didn't* want. "I wanted to be a businessman in California," they may say, "and here I am a missionary in the boonies of Africa." The implication is that commitment to Christ leads to second best. But God never gives second best to His followers—even though from our limited perspective we may think this is what we have received. God always gives what is best for us when we yield our personal ambitions to him.

Personal Possessions

Thirdly, discipleship may cost us our *possessions*. Riches, health, fame, material goods—none of these is wrong in itself, and often God gives these things in abundance, but they become wrong when they are made the chief ends in life.

Recently my wife and I were in the market for another house. We had clearly outgrown our old home and felt the need for more space. One evening we made a list of everything we wanted: fireplace, dishwasher, separate dining room, attached garage, etc. To quote one friend, we were looking for "a champagne house on a beer budget!"

Before long we began to ask why we wanted a larger house at all. Were we being pulled into the standards of a culture which measures success by the size of one's house or the make and model of one's car? Were we being caught up into a way of thinking which measures personal worth by the abundance of our possessions? Our house-hunting reminded us that in eternity a person's value will not be measured by what he or she possessed on earth. All of our possessions, including our money, homes, automobiles, and labor-saving gadgets, come from the hand of God. All belong to God, must be surrendered to God, and should be used in ways which ultimately enable us to be better disciples of Jesus Christ and disciplers of others. A striving for personal possessions and the adherence to a secular lifestyle can hinder our effectiveness in obeying Christ's Great Commission.

THE RESPONSIBILITIES OF DISCIPLESHIP

In addition to these costs, being a disciple involves three responsibilities.

Witnessing for Christ

First, the disciple is responsible to *witness for Christ*. This does not mean withdrawing from all nonbelievers; it means that by following Paul's example we must search for common ground with non-Christians, ultimately hoping to lead some men to Christ (1 Cor. 9:19-22).

> The ministry of a disciple is the ministry of introducing Jesus Christ to men who do not know Him. The ministry of a disciple is the ministry of imparting to others the truth concerning the Father and the Son that has been revealed to us by the Holy Spirit. The ministry of a disciple makes one a channel through which the Spirit of God brings divine truth home to men who are ignorant of God because of their natural blindness.
>
> Men are not disciples because of what they give or what they do.
>
> They are disciples because of what they communicate to others about Jesus Christ . . . . We carry out the ministry of a disciple in two principal ways, by our lives and by our lips. One without the other is insufficient and inadequate. The Word of God that comes from the lips of the disciple must be corroborated by the works of God in the life of the disciple.[5]

Bringing Others to Maturity

A second responsibility of the disciple is to *bring others to maturity*. Paul wrote about this in his Letter to the Colossians (1:28, 29). Paul was the instrument of the Holy Spirit, and he acknowledged that God provides the necessary power and then works through committed human beings to bring other persons to a state of spiritual maturity.

It has been suggested that there are five ways by which we stimulate maturation in others: by serving as an example of what mature Christianity should be like (1 Thes. 2:8), by providing opportunities for a disciple to have practical experiences in witnessing and serving (Mark 6:7), by evaluating the disciple's actions during his period of training (Mark 6:30), by teaching and giving information (2 Tim. 3:15-17), and by honestly confronting others with the difficulties of discipleship (Luke 14:25-33).[6] These five principles can be used as we disciple others, and they can be used by the people who disciple us. Perhaps these are also some of the ways in which God makes us into the kinds of individuals that He wants us to be.

Making Disciplers

Finally, the disciple has the responsibility of *making disciplers*—training those who can go forth to disciple others. Paul outlined this very explicitly when writing to Timothy: "My son, be strong in the grace that is in Christ Jesus. And the things which you have heard from me in the presence of many witnesses, these entrust to faithful men, who will be able to teach others also" (2 Tim. 2:1, 2). Discipleship is a multiplication process in which those who are disciples disciple others, who in turn become disciplers. God never intended Christians to accept the gospel and then do nothing further. He intended that we should become His disciples, with all of the characteristics, costs, and responsibilities that this involves, and then go forth to make additional disciples for Christ.

DISCIPLESHIP AND PEOPLE HELPING

The emphasis on discipleship is so central to the teachings of the New Testament and so basic to the Christian way of life that it would be impossible to ignore it whenever the Christian enters a counseling or other helping relationship. The counselor is dealing with people in need, and the Christian counselor who overlooks or sidesteps the Biblical message in such a situation is directly turning his back on the teachings of Jesus. Discipleship must be a part of the Christian counselor's life, and it must be one of his prime concerns when he enters into a helping relationship with another human being.

The counselor who takes the Great Commission seriously will differ from the non-Christian helper in several ways. First, the believer will recognize that the place to start helping is with the helper's own life. Not only must the helper look at his or her own psychological hangups and attempt to change (perhaps with the help of another counselor), but there must also be a spiritual self-examination. "Am I really committed to Christ?" the helper must ask. "Am I sensitive to the Spirit's leading, seeking to purge sin from my life, growing as a disciple of Jesus Christ, and being sincerely interested in the spiritual growth of others?" It is possible to answer no to each of these questions and still help people; successful secular therapists demonstrate this every day. But counseling which leaves out the spiritual dimension is ultimately futile. It may build treasures on earth for the helper but it does nothing to prepare helpees for eternity or to help them experience the abundant life on earth—an abundance which comes only with commitment to Christ (John 10:10).

The disciple of Jesus Christ hopes ultimately that his helpees will grow in their commitment to and knowledge of Jesus Christ. This is not to imply that evangelism and spiritual maturing are the *only* goals of counseling, but they are crucially important goals which even Christians often overlook.

THREE APPROACHES TO COUNSELING

In addition, the Christian helper must take a different view of the whole helping process. Consider, for example, three broad counseling approaches frequently used today. Only one of these is truly Biblical.[7]

Humanistic-Secular Approach

The *humanistic-secular* approach to counseling provides no place for God. In this approach, the counselee moves toward goals which improve his personal well-being, and the counselor intervenes for a while to help with the achievement of these goals.

"God as Helper" Approach

In contrast, there is some counseling which might be labeled the *"God as helper"* approach. Here the goal is still the same but God is seen as a helper and perhaps even a cotherapist who, in response to prayer, helps the counselor and counselee in their work.

Theocentric Approach

Very different is what might be termed the *theocentric* approach. This assumes that an eternal God exists who has ultimate purposes for mankind. In counseling, God comes into a relationship and uses the counselor as His instrument to bring changes in the counselee's life. These changes hopefully restore harmony between the counselee and his God, improve his personal relationships with others, reduce his inner conflicts, and instill the peace that passes understanding.

The disciple who is also a helper strives for this theocentric approach. Empowered by the Holy Spirit, he is willing to develop the characteristics, pay the costs, and bear the responsibilities of discipleship. In turn, he becomes God's instrument for bringing changes in the lives of those with whom he counsels.

THE FLEXIBILITY OF BIBLICAL COUNSELING

It is unrealistic to expect that we will ever arrive at one Biblical approach to counseling, any more than we have discovered one Biblical approach to missions, evangelism, or preaching. To a large extent, counseling techniques depend on the personality of the counselor and the nature of the counselee's problems, but we should seek to uncover the various techniques and several counseling approaches which arise out of or are clearly consistent with the teachings of Scripture. Then we should try out these techniques and test their effectiveness, not using subjective feelings as proof that we are "really helping people," but employing carefully controlled evaluation and assessment techniques.

The place to begin building a Christian approach to counseling is with the Bible, and there can be no more basic starting place than the Great Commission given by Jesus Himself. This is a blueprint for building the church, and it forms a basis on which to build lives and interpersonal relationships by helping people through counseling.

2
THE BASICS OF PEOPLE HELPING

What is a Christian people helper? Does the Christian have different goals in helping than the nonbeliever? If he or she takes the Bible seriously, will this influence how the helper deals with his helpees? Can there be a Biblical approach to counseling which allows for the individual personality differences of helpers, the uniqueness of each helpee, and the variety of problems that are encountered in a helping situation? Must a Christian helper throw out all the counseling theories and techniques that secular therapists have developed and shown to be effective? Is there a uniquely Christian approach to counseling help?

These were some of the questions which concerned me several years ago when I received my doctorate in clinical psychology and went to work in a university counseling center. I had a diploma to prove that I was trained as a counselor, but I didn't feel very competent in spite of all my education at some very reputable graduate schools. As a Christian it seemed that I ought to be doing something more than just rigorously following the secular methods that I had been taught, but I didn't know how to do anything that was both different and better. Employed in the counseling center of a state university, I couldn't say much about religion to my counselees and still keep my job, but I also knew that the gospel of Jesus Christ had something to say to these lonely and frustrated kids who were coming to my office. Often I thought back to a paper that I had written as a class assignment in graduate school. The paper was titled ''The Effectiveness of Psychotherapy,'' and in it I concluded (after reviewing a great deal of published research) that counseling didn't work very well. Obviously this conclusion didn't do much to boost my morale as a young psychologist just out of graduate school!

THE PRIORITY OF PEOPLE HELPING

During my year in that counseling center I think I helped a lot of people, and my employer appeared to be happy with my work. But I wasn't satisfied. After several months on the job I decided that teaching was more my gift, and so I left the counseling center and went to work in the psychology department of a growing liberal arts college. Teaching was a very rewarding experience, but I still harbored my insecurities about counseling. Then I met Paul Tournier, the famous Swiss writer, and for the first time I began to see something of the potential of Christian counseling.

Tournier is a humble, godly man who has helped thousands of people through his counseling and his books. We may not agree with all of Dr. Tournier's conclusions, but in writing a book about this man[1] I saw an individual whose counseling is effective. As a people helper, he takes the Bible seriously, is compassionate, consistently demonstrates Christian love, and recognizes that every helper is in some way unique. Although Tournier has not proposed a formal system of Biblical counseling, he has nevertheless developed a basically Biblical approach to counseling.

But other writers have proposed different approaches which also claim to be Biblical. This confuses a lot of people. How can we be Christians, they ask, and have such a variety of counseling systems, all of which claim to come from the Bible? We need to remember that counselors, like theologians and Bible students, are fallible human beings. We see things from different perspectives. Committed Presbyterians disagree with committed Baptists on some important issues—yet all may be Christian. There are different Biblically based approaches to preaching (homiletics) or Bible interpretation (hermeneutics), even though each may be faithful to the Word of God. The same is true in counseling. Because of these differences, we learn from each other, recognizing that men will never have the perfect theory of counseling until we get to heaven, and then counseling will no longer be necessary!

THE PRIORITY OF THE GREAT COMMISSION

So long as we remain on earth, however, if we are to take the Bible seriously in our counseling, we cannot ignore the Great Commission. To do so would be to leave out a major tenet of New Testament teaching. So important, in fact, is the concept of discipleship in Scripture that we might think of Christian counseling as *discipleship counseling.*

Discipleship counseling is an approach which is built on Scripture—which begins with the Bible as its starting point. It is a view of counseling which recognizes the centrality of the Great Commission and has the discipling of others at its core. It assumes that the God who speaks through the Bible has also revealed truth about His universe through science, including psychology. Thus, psychological methods and techniques are taken seriously, but they must be tested, not only scientifically and pragmatically, but primarily against the written Word of God. Discipleship counseling uses a variety of methods which depend on the counselor's personality and skill and on the counselee's needs, personality, or problems. The goals of counseling are to help people function more effectively in their daily lives; to find freedom from spiritual, psychological, and interpersonal conflicts; to be at peace with themselves and to enjoy a growing communion with God; to develop and maintain smooth interpersonal relations with others; to realize their fullest potential in Christ; and to be actively involved in becoming disciples of and disciplers for Jesus Christ.

THE PRINCIPLES OF PEOPLE HELPING

The discipleship approach to counseling is expressed in terms of six general principles, which I will refer to as "people helping principles." Three of them are presented in this chapter and three in the next chapter.

People Helping Principle 1

In any helping relationship, the personality, values, attitudes, and beliefs of the helper are of primary importance. In writing to the church at Galatia, Paul instructed the brethren to "restore" (bring to a state of wholeness) any individual who was having personal difficulties (Gal. 6:1). Apparently some of the Galatians were lapsing into sin and were having problems because of this. These men and women were of concern to the Apostle, but notice who was to help them: "you who are spiritual."

In chapter 5 of Galatians we read the well-known listing of those traits that characterize the spiritual Christian: love, joy, peace, patience, kindness, goodness, faithfulness, gentleness, and self-control (Gal. 5:22, 23). The spiritual individual is the person who brings his values into conformity with the teachings of Jesus (Gal. 5:24), is led by the Spirit of God (v. 25), and is not self-centered, a troublemaker, or impressed with his own importance (v. 26).

In addition, notice that the Biblical helper is gentle (Gal. 6:1), a person who may be firm with the helpee but is also compassionate. He is alert to the temptations that come when one is involved in an intimate counseling relationship (v. 1), and is involved with people (v. 2), so much so that the helper for a time bears the helpee's burdens with the pain and inconvenience that this might bring. The Biblical helper is humble (v. 3), recognizing the source of his strength and not acting in a superior, holier-than-thou manner. He is self-examining (v. 4) (involved in realistic self-appraisal and avoiding comparisons with others), responsible for bearing burdens in his own life (v. 5), inclined to assist others in doing the same, and willing to learn from the helpee (v. 6). The Biblical helper is aware of God and of spiritual influences in human behavior (vv. 7, 8) and is patient (v. 9) even when the helping task is long and arduous. He recognizes a responsibility to do good to all people but "especially to those who are of the household of faith" (v. 10).

This is a long and somewhat overwhelming list. The standards for a good helper are high, but they are attainable. These standards should characterize any Christian who is walking in close fellowship with Jesus Christ. However, it does not follow that every committed believer is automatically a good counselor, since the learning of specific skills is important too. But the person who follows Jesus Christ develops characteristics that might be summarized in the one little word *love*, and this is crucially important in people helping.

All of this is consistent with psychological research on the counseling relationship, research which shows that the personal traits of the helper are as important to good counseling as are the methods which he uses.[2] Several research studies have shown that effective counselors succeed not so much because of their theoretical orientation or techniques but because of their empathy, warmth, and genuineness.

Empathy comes from the German word *einfülung*, which means "to feel into" or "to feel with." Most of us have had the experience of sitting in the passenger's seat of a car, pushing our foot on the floor when we see the need to slow down. At such times we are feeling into the driver's situation and are feeling with him.

In counseling, the effective helper tries to see and understand the problem from the helpee's perspective. "Why is he so upset?" we might ask. "How does he view the situation?" "If I were him, how would I feel?" As helpers we need to keep our own objective viewpoints intact, but we also need to realize that we can be of greatest help if we can in addition see the problem from the helpee's point of view and can let him know that we understand how he feels and views his situation. The helpee, in turn, needs to realize that someone is really trying to understand. This mutual understanding builds maximum rapport between the helper and the helpee.

Warmth is somewhat synonymous with caring. It is friendliness and consideration shown by facial expression, tone of voice, gestures, posture, eye-contact, and such non-verbal behavior as looking after the helpee's comfort. Warmth says, "I care about you and your well-being." Here, as in so much human behavior, actions speak louder than words. The helper who really cares about people won't have to advertise his concern verbally. Everyone will be able to see it.

Genuineness means that the helper's words are consistent with his actions. He or she tries to be honest with the helpee, avoiding any statement or behavior which could be considered phony or insincere. According to one writer[3] the truly genuine person is spontaneous but not impulsive or disrespectful, consistent in his values or attitudes, not defensive, aware of his own emotions, and willing to share of himself and his own feelings.

Jesus showed empathy, warmth, and genuineness, and the successful Christian helper must do the same. It is possible, however, that each of these can be overdone. We can show so much empathy that we lose our objectivity, so much warmth that the helpee feels smothered, and so much genuineness that the helper loses sight of the helpee's needs. The helper, therefore, must frequently examine his own motives for helping. As helpers, our own needs will be met in the helping relationship, but our primary task is to help others with their problems and struggles.

People Helping Principle 2

The helpee's attitudes, motivation, and desire for help are also important in counseling. At some time most counselors have had the frustrating experience of trying to work with someone who is stubborn, uncooperative, or not interested in changing his behavior. To work with a rebellious teenager who has been sent to be "straightened out" or to counsel a depressed person who believes that he or she "will never get better" is to work with a person whose attitude will have to change before real helping can occur. When the helpee does not want help, fails to see that a problem exists, has no desire to change, or lacks faith in the helper and the helping process, then counseling is rarely successful. God created us with a free will, and it is no more possible to help an unwilling helpee to grow psychologically than it is to help a nonbeliever to grow spiritually against his will. In counseling, as in witnessing, such resistance must be acknowledged and the helpee must be helped to see the value in making changes in his own life. Counseling is a process of assisting another person to change and grow, but such growth is easiest when the helper and helpee work together on the task. In one sense the helpee is the best-informed individual in the world when it comes to his own situation. He knows how he feels and what has *not* worked in bringing about change in the past. The helper and helpee must both use this information together.

Of course, it should not be assumed that the person who needs help is always resisting in a stubborn manner. Sometimes people are simply afraid. It is often hard for a person to talk about his failures or problems, and sometimes the helpee doesn't even know what is wrong. To tell someone else about our personal life can be risky, since we might be criticized or rejected. Then there is the attitude of frustration or self-condemnation which some helpees feel because they haven't been able to solve their problems on their own. All of these can interfere with the helping process, and thus the helper's job is to help the helpee relax and "open up."

For best results, the counselee-helpee must really want to change, must expect that things will get better with the counselor's help, and must show a willingness to cooperate even if the counseling process is painful. Stated somewhat differently, it is important for the helpee to have or get an attitude of hope when he or she comes for help.

Jesus emphasized the value of this in His healing ministry. He commended the hemorrhaging woman for a faith which restored her to health (Mark 5:34), He healed two blind men because of their faith (Matt. 9:29), and He cured an epileptic boy whose father believed in the Master's powers (Mark 9:23-27). In contrast, when Jesus was in His hometown, not very many people were helped because they didn't believe in His healing powers (Matt. 13:58). It could be argued, perhaps, that faith as described in the Scriptures is different from hope and expectation, but the writer of the Hebrews links them together (Heb. 11:1). Terms like faith, hope, expectation, belief, and motivation can all be used somewhat interchangeably because they all convey the idea that when a helpee desires to improve and thinks that he will get better, he very often does get better—sometimes in spite of the helper and his or her techniques.

People Helping Principle 3

The helping relationship between helper and helpee is of great significance. As every counseling student soon learns, good rapport is essential for successful counseling, so essential that one writer has even described counseling as primarily a helping relationship between two or more people.[4] Sometimes we call this relationship a counseling interview, a therapy session, an encounter, or a "good talk between friends," but in every case people are together in some kind of a relationship in which they work together on one or more problems.

Helping relationships differ both in their nature and depth. When two people come together they do not leave their personalities, values, attitudes, insecurities, needs, feelings, perceptions, and abilities at the door. All of these enter into the relationship, and to the extent that people are different, it is likely that no two people ever relate together in a way that is duplicated elsewhere. Consider, for example, how Jesus related to people. He didn't have the same kind of relationship with all of them. With Nicodemus it was intellectual, with the Pharisees it was confrontational, with Mary and Martha it was more relaxed, and with little children it was warm and loving. Jesus recognized individual differences in personality, needs, and level of understanding, and He treated people accordingly. When counselors try to treat all of their counselees in the same way, they fail to build good rapport because they are making the mistake of thinking that all people are alike. All people are *not* alike, and this must be recognized both in the relationships that we build and in the methods that we use.

Jesus not only dealt with people in different ways, but He also related to individuals at different levels of depth or closeness. John was the disciple whom Jesus loved, perhaps the Master's nearest friend, while Peter, James, and John together appear to have comprised an inner circle with whom the Lord had a special relationship. Although they were not as close as the inner three, the other apostles were Christ's constant companions, a band of twelve men who had been handpicked to carry on the work after Christ's departure. In Luke 10 we read of a group of seventy men to whom Jesus gave special training. Following the resurrection He appeared to a larger group of five hundred people, and then there were crowds, sometimes numbering in the thousands, many of whom may have seen Christ only once and from a distance.

The closeness of Jesus to His disciples might be illustrated by the diagram on the following page. Jesus is in the center. John, His closest friend, is at 1, the Peter-James-John trio is next in nearness (2), then the twelve (3), then the seventy (4), then the five hundred (5), and finally the crowds (6) at the outer reaches of the circle.

Most of us have this kind of relationship with others. Some people are close while others are farther removed. We sometimes assume that in counseling or discipling we must always develop a close relationship, but in fact it may be that such relationships can be deep or not-so-deep.

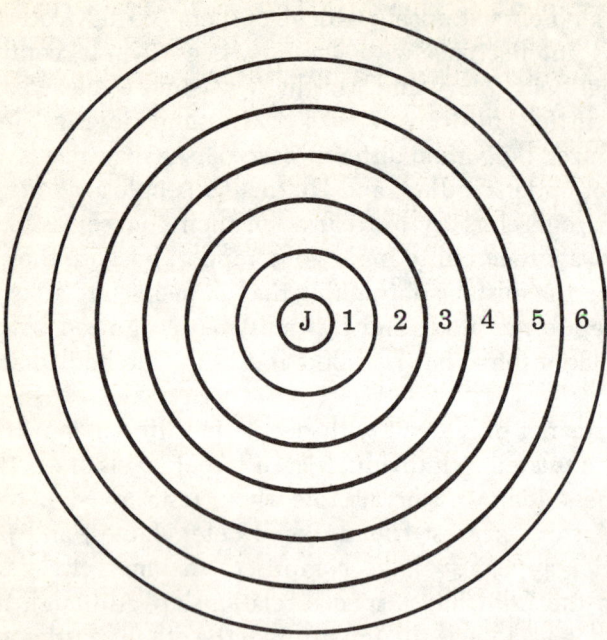

Consider, for example, the different degrees of closeness that a teacher might have with his students. As a follower of Jesus Christ, I have an inescapable obligation to make disciples for the Master from my students and counselees, but I approach these people in different ways and I am closer to some than to others. At number 1 in the diagram is my graduate assistant, with whom I meet almost daily. He works for me part-time, helps with my courses or research, and studies under my direction. At times we pray together, share together, and have lunch with each other. Sometimes he observes as I relax at home with my family, and at other times he sees me when I am under pressure trying to meet some deadline. We have discussed freely some of his conflicts and problems, but I have also been open with him about my personal concerns and struggles. In many respects our relationship is similar to what Paul had in mind when he wrote to Timothy, "My son, be strong in the grace that is in Christ Jesus. And the things which you have heard from me . . . these entrust to faithful men, who will be able to teach others also" (2 Timothy 2:1, 2). In the past, I have had graduate assistants who work in the dormitory of a nearby Christian college. As resident advisors they are involved in teaching others some of the things they have been learning from me.

As a professor, however, there are other students whom I disciple. Like Peter, James, and John (at number 2 in the diagram) there are a few students with whom I have a close relationship and with whom I meet frequently. My group of academic advisees might parallel the twelve disciples (number 3). Twice a week I meet with these men and women. We pray regularly for each other, and one is always with me when I go speaking within driving distance of my home. Less intimate is my relationship with the seventy or so students who enroll in my classes each quarter. We meet a few times each week for ten weeks and then go our separate ways. Even less involved is my relationship with the whole student body, some of whom meet me casually on campus or hear me speak in chapel but have no other contact with me. Then there are those at number 6 in the diagram, the people who may hear me speak or read a book like this one but have no closer contact with me.

As disciplers it seems that each one of us is surrounded by circles of people. A few, perhaps one or two friends and the members of our family, are very close. Others are a little farther removed, and some are on the outer fringes touched only casually by our witness for Christ. To fulfill the Great Commission, each of us at the centers of our circles of influence must first of all be disciples of Jesus Christ who are completely committed to Him and obedient to His direction for our lives. Then in interpersonal relations— teaching, counseling, parenting, indeed in all of our activities—we must be witnesses for Christ, reaching out to others close and far and showing them by word and deed what it means to be a disciple and a discipler.

Such discipleship isn't easy. It involves dedication to Christ, a willingness to be open to others, and a flexibility in our relationships with the people around us. But to be a disciple and discipler is the responsibility of every Christian and it starts where we are—at the center of our own series of circles.

The same series of circles could also characterize our helping relationships. The helper need not necessarily strive to be the helpee's best friend. Counseling is a relationship that certainly may involve friendship, but it exists primarily for another purpose—to have the helper assist the counselee with a problem. At times the relationship may be very close, near the center of the circle, with intimate, even two-way, sharing of emotions, concerns, and needs. On other occasions the relationship may not be as deep. Perhaps the helper and helpee see each other for one session, talk about the helpee only, or chat briefly about some relatively minor problem. It is even possible for the helper to help others from a distance—by giving a public lecture on mental health, for example, or writing a helpful book. Sometimes, therefore, we help people on a one-to-one basis in an office, sometimes we work in a group, and at times we may even help people whom we never meet face-to-face.

Every helper-helpee relationship is in some sense unique. Each relationship depends on the personality of the people involved, the nature of the problems being considered, the depth of discussion, and the psychological closeness of the helper to the person being helped. Counseling is a helping process, but the helping involves a relationship. The better the relationship, the more successful the counseling.

3
THE TECHNIQUES OF PEOPLE HELPING

Effective helping, as we have indicated, has at least six basic principles, three of which were discussed in the previous chapter. There first must be a helper who shows empathy, warmth, and genuineness. Second, there must be a helpee who is motivated to change and is willing to work with the helper to solve problems. Third, good counseling requires a helper-helpee relationship which may or may not be close but which exists for the purpose of helping people to get along better with themselves, with each other, and with God.

The above paragraph would have distressed both Freud and a great many more contemporary counselors. Freud placed considerable emphasis on the counselor's skills, and to some extent this is right. It would be wrong to conclude that two warm, loving people who have a smooth relationship are the only requirements for good counseling. These are basics, but successful counseling involves more. It involves skills and techniques which good counselors learn, practice, and constantly refine. It is true, of course, that some people seem to have a "feel" for counseling. They apparently are successful even without training or study in counseling procedures. But with training and awareness of technique, even these people can be more effective in the helping relationship.

One of the skills needed by a helper is an awareness of how the helpee feels, what he is thinking, and how his own actions may be influencing the problem. This brings us to the fourth of the six principles which we began describing in the preceding chapter.

People Helping Principle 4

Helping must focus on the helpee's emotions, thoughts, and behavior—all three. In many of the secular and Christian approaches to counseling there is an emphasis on either emotion, or thinking, or behavior, but rarely on all three together. Albert Ellis's Rational Emotive Therapy, for example, refers to both thinking and feeling in its title, but the therapy almost exclusively deals with how the counselee *thinks*. In contrast, Carl Rogers puts most emphasis on the *feelings* of the counselee and makes little attempt to analyze what is happening to him intellectually. Many of the learning approaches emphasize behavior change and maintain that the counselee's feelings and thoughts are of minor importance—so minor, in fact, that "treatment" sometimes occurs without the counselee's even being aware that it is taking place.

When we look into Scripture we see that feeling, thinking, and behavior are all of great, perhaps equal, importance. Consider, first, the emotional aspects. Jesus Himself wept on at least two occasions and sometimes got angry. He did not deny feelings, nor did He condemn people for experiencing and expressing their emotions. Clearly He was sensitive to the feelings of others, such as His sorrowing mother at the time of the crucifixion or the parents who brought their children to see the Lord but were rebuffed by the overprotective disciples. It is possible to overemphasize feelings in a counseling relationship, but it is also possible to stifle or deny them. Jesus did neither.

There were times, however, when He put more emphasis on rational thinking. Thomas was very much inclined to doubt, but Jesus dealt with these intellectual questions in a rational way. He did not ignore Thomas or criticize him for a lack of faith. Instead, when the disciples doubted, Jesus supplied the evidence. Following the resurrection Thomas had said, in essence, "I won't believe unless I can see with my eyes and touch the hands of Jesus with my fingers." As they met later, the Lord said to

Thomas, "Reach here your finger and see my hands; and reach here your hand and put it into my side; and be not unbelieving, but believing" (John 20:27). In a similar way, when John the Baptist doubted during his last days in prison (Matt. 11:2-6), Jesus provided the rational facts which were needed. On numerous occasions He carried on intellectual debates with the religious leaders of His day; for example, He discussed apologetics with Nicodemus in a debate which may have gone far into the night.

But Jesus was also very concerned about sin and sinful behavior. He told the woman taken in adultery to change her behavior and to sin no more, He instructed Mary to change her hectic life-style, He advised the rich young ruler to be less selfish, and He told two quarreling brothers to stop being so greedy. Repeatedly in His sermons and discussions with individuals Jesus confronted people with their sinful, self-centered behavior and instructed them to change.

The emphasis on emotions, thinking, and behavior is seen in the Book of Acts and on through the New Testament epistles. Repeatedly believers are held responsible for their own actions, but there is never any hint of overemphasizing behavior to the exclusion of feeling and thinking.

At the end of his Letter to the Philippians, the Apostle Paul gives a great deal of practical advice for daily living. First he deals with the emotions, instructing his readers to rejoice, to be patient, to be nonanxious, and to be calmed by the peace of God (Phil. 4:4-7). Then there is an emphasis on thinking. "Let your mind dwell . . ." we are told, on those things which are true, honorable, right, pure, lovely, good, excellent, and praiseworthy (Phil. 4:8). Finally there is emphasis on behavior. We should practice what we have been taught, learn like Paul to be content and do all things in the power of Christ (Phil. 4:9-13). Feeling, thinking, and acting—all three are important in the Scriptures and each must be considered in counseling. As shown in the diagram on the following page,[1] each is in contact with the

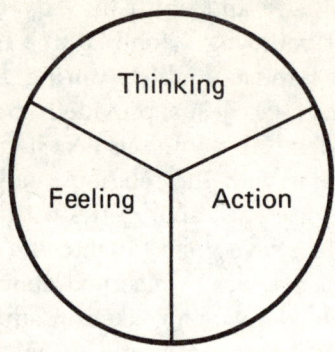

others. When we have emotional problems, for example, our thinking and actions are affected. We cannot emphasize one part of this diagram while we ignore the other two parts.

People Helping Principle 5

Helping involves a variety of helper skills. This word "skills" might be viewed from two perspectives. On the one hand there are the counseling techniques—things like listening attentively, watching carefully, or questioning wisely as the helpee describes his problem. These refer to *what one does* in counseling. They are skills which can be learned by the counselor-helper.

For maximum effectiveness, counseling must also have direction. Both helper and helpee must have some goals in mind, and at least the helper should have some idea about how these goals can be reached. This moving toward a goal might be called the process of counseling. It refers to *where one goes* in a helping relationship.

Numerous books have been written to describe counseling techniques. The list of techniques varies from author to author, but most writers agree that in order to understand and help another human being the helper must at least make use of the following:

a) *Listening.* This involves giving our undivided attention to the helpee and showing this attention through eye contact, a relaxed posture, the use of encouraging statements (e.g., "that makes good sense," "I see what you mean"), an occasional probing response (e.g., "go on," "tell me more," "what then?"), and a periodic repeating of what the helpee said, just to be sure we understand.

Even with His perfect knowledge of people's inner personality and problems (John 2:25), Jesus listened patiently (Luke 24:13-24). Perhaps in so doing He was showing that there is therapeutic value in letting an individual put his troubles into words that can be shared with another (James 5:16). In listening, we who are helpers must not get angry, but must show by our attentive attitude that we really want to share the helpee's burdens with him (James 1:19; Gal. 6:2).

An unwillingness to listen can sometimes be a great obstacle to helping. This is true in evangelism as well as in counseling. If the Christian is always talking he is not able to respond to the personal problems or needs of the person to whom he is speaking. Sometimes that person has some question to ask or some problem to discuss before he can commit his life to Christ or grow further as a believer. If we don't give him a chance to express himself we are in danger of undermining our own attempts at helping.[2]

Table 1 on the following page lists some general suggestions for making our listening more helpful to others. In reading this it should not be assumed that our only task is to listen to everything that is said. Our task as helpers is to understand the helpee and show by our listening that we care. It is not our job, however, to develop an expertise in understanding the details of other people's sins. There is a place for innocence and purity on the part of the helper (Matt. 10:16), and at times we may need to say "I think I'm getting the picture, so I probably don't need to hear all of the details of your situation." Be careful, however, that you don't intervene with such a statement too quickly. It could stifle discussion and cut you off from information which

Some Guidelines for Listening

1. *Prepare to listen.*

    1) Intellectually: Reading about the issue being discussed can help you to listen both intelligently and critically. To know what to listen for is to listen better. Don't avoid difficult subjects.

    2) Physically: Since listening is hard work, take enough rest before you face it. Don't take an overrelaxed position that induces fatigue or grogginess.

    3) Mentally:

        a. Realize that if you really want to listen to another person, this will do a great deal to increase your listening effectiveness.

        b. Decide that you are going to learn by listening. Daniel Webster once said that by listening to intelligent men he had learned more than from reading books. Listening is not only one of the best ways of learning new information and ideas, but it is also one of the best ways of learning about people—those to whom you listen.

        c. Be aware that concentration is not easy and that listening requires discipline.

        d. Recognize that not-listening equals indifference, and this doesn't help anyone.

        e. Realize that learning to listen to one another helps us learn how to listen to God.

        f. Get rid of the idea that listening is less important than speaking. A poor listener is likely to be a poor speaker as well.

        g. Don't assume that you already know the full implications of the idea you are listening to.

2. *Judge content as well as delivery.* We look at the speaker and often concentrate on what we see rather

---

*Adapted from Masaki Kakitani, "Listening Evangelism" (unpublished manuscript presented to Trinity Evangelical Divinity School, Deerfield, Illinois, December 1973).

TABLE 1 — continued

than on what we hear. We can better understand content by paying attention to both nonverbal and verbal cues from the speaker.

3. *Control your emotions.* You might feel overpowered by your own emotional problems and be tempted to stop listening intently. Don't stop listening because you dislike the other person. Be patient with what he says.

4. *Resist distractions.* We are distracted not only by what we hear, but by what we see and are thinking. A good listener instinctively fights such distractions.

5. *Pay attention.* Attention is necessary for listening. Try to be interested in what is being said. Look at the person who is talking. Lean toward the person as he or she talks.

6. *Capitalize on the fact that you can think faster than another person can talk.*
   1) Think ahead.
   2) Weigh what you hear.
   3) Review what you have heard.
   4) Listen between the lines.

7. *Ask questions sparingly.* Especially try to avoid asking "why?"

8. *Try not to interrupt.*

9. *Stick to the speaker's subject.*

10. *Use the speaker's words to get your own point across.*

11. *Don't preach.*

12. *Go slow on giving advice.* Most people don't want advice and promptly ignore it when they hear it.

13. *Don't argue.* Don't try to persuade your helpee by becoming more argumentative, for this confirms his original beliefs and leaves him deaf to any kind of reasoning about the subject. If you win the argument you may lose a friend. If you lose, you may forfeit the respect of your helpee. Either way you have nothing to gain, and neither does your helpee.

14. *Don't probe for additional facts for your own curiosity.* Your purpose is not that of obtaining information for yourself.

could be helpful in your people helping, even though you personally are not edified by your hearing.

b) *Leading*. Sometimes we use techniques which encourage the counselee to talk. We want him to share his feelings, to say what he is thinking, and to describe what he has done or not done about the problem.

Perhaps there are few things more frustrating, especially for the novice counselor, than a helpee who clams up and refuses to talk. At such times we might ask a question which can *not* be answered by a simple yes or no ("What are you thinking about right now?" "Tell me more about your parents." "Can you give me an example of not getting along with your wife?") We might summarize his or her situation as we see it, just to be sure we understand correctly; we might make a leading comment ("What happened next?" "Where did you go from there?" "What do you think will happen to you now?"); or we might use a technique which psychologists call reflecting.

Reflecting involves saying in fresh words what the helpee seems to be feeling ("That must have made you feel good!", "It seems like she made you pretty mad," or "Sounds to me like you feel pretty guilty over what you did"). Reflecting can also involve the restatement of thoughts ("Am I picking up the fact that you're not sure of yourself on a date?", "Does this mean that you don't understand your teacher?") or a description of behavior ("Right now you seem to be pretty tense," "You're smiling but I get the idea that you really hurt inside"). After any of these responses, the helpee should be given the opportunity to respond—even if this consists of telling the helper that he or she has missed the point completely.

As we use leading responses, our goal is to stimulate the helpee to state his feelings or thoughts and to encourage an honest look at his behavior. The purpose is not so much to get information for ourselves as to help the counselee clarify his or her problem. It is then that he can move to the point of getting some new insight or taking some action that will bring about change.

Jesus used leading comments when He walked along with those two discouraged men on the road to Emmaus. "What are these words that you are exchanging with one another as you are walking?" He asked. When Cleopas described the recent things that had taken place in Jerusalem, Jesus said, "What things?" (Luke 24:17-19). These were leading questions which got the men talking.

c) *Supporting.* This word in no way implies that the helper holds up psychological cripples so that they never learn to cope with their problems alone. Support does recognize, however, that it is difficult for a helpee to open up, to talk about failures, to admit sinful thoughts and actions, or to acknowledge that some problem has him defeated. To talk openly—especially to a Christian counselor—is to risk being rejected, criticized, or ostracized. This is why people often keep their failures and inner thoughts to themselves. If we tell others they might think less of us or even turn away from us. This fear of rejection is at the basis of so much of the phony behavior that is seen in our society.

The Bible tells us, however, that we should confess our faults, not only to God in prayer, but also to one another (James 5:16). In hearing such confessions the helper's reaction must not be shock and rejection, but neither do we condone sinful behavior or pretend that it is unimportant. The Christian sympathetically bears the helpee's burdens with him (Gal. 6:2; Rom. 15:1). At times we rejoice with the helpee over some victory, but at other times we may even weep with him (Rom. 12:15). If there is sin we encourage the helpee to confess it, and we stick with him as he works at changing his attitudes or behavior. We are giving emotional and spiritual support as the helpee takes steps to personal maturity and growth.

d) *Confronting.* It is possible for the helper to listen, to make leading comments, and to support a helpee who nevertheless doesn't get better at all. This is because the helpee's problem is often rooted in behavior, attitudes, or thoughts which must be changed. For such change to occur, the helpee must face up to his or her actions, and the helper must help this process along with a firm but gentle confrontation.

Jesus did a great deal of confrontation. He confronted the Pharisees with their hypocrisy, the disciples with their lack of understanding, Martha with her excessive busyness, and the rich young ruler with his misplaced values. It seems, in fact, that confrontation was a central part of Jesus' dealings with others. It was a technique which carried over into the early church and was seen most clearly when Paul confronted Peter with his cowardly capitulation to the demands of the so-called Judaizers (Gal. 2:1-21).

Confrontation involves the pointing out of sin in a helpee's life, but it is not limited to this. We can confront helpees with their inconsistent behavior ("You say you love your wife, but you are mean to her." "You claim to like sports but you never play") or with their self-defeating behavior ("You want to succeed, but you set your standards so high that you are sure to fail") or with their tendency to evade issues ("You say you want to grow spiritually, but every time this issue comes up you change the subject").

Confrontation is a difficult task. It must be done in a gentle and nonjudgmental fashion (Gal. 6:1; Matt. 7:1), but the helper must be courageous enough to risk bearing the overt or passive resistance of a helpee who may not want to face the reality of sin or inconsistency in his life. Remember that the helper's task is not to condemn but to *help*, not to stir up trouble but to *heal*. Sometimes, however, healing must be preceded by painful surgery. Recognize therefore that the helpee may feel threatened when he is confronted. The helper should therefore give support even as he confronts, and he must give ample opportunity for the helpee to respond to the confrontation, either by expressing his reactions or altering his behavior. In helping we are working *together* on a problem, more or less as a team of equals—not as a counselor-judge who lords it over the counselee-victim.

e) *Teaching.* Basically this is what counseling really is.

The helpee is learning how to act, feel, and think differently; the helper is fulfilling the role of a teacher.

Teaching, of course, can occur in a variety of ways. It may involve instruction, giving advice, or telling the helpee what to do. Very often, however, such verbal direction has little impact on a helpee. It is usually more effective for a helper to show by his behavior how to live or think more effectively; to give praise, encouragement, or other reinforcement when the helpee shows improvement; and to work with the helpee as he makes decisions, takes actions, and evaluates what he is doing to change.

All of these helping techniques describe what the counselor-helper does in his counseling, but equally important is the question of goals. Where is the counseling going and what does it seek to accomplish? All of this refers to the process of helping.

This is a big topic of debate among professional counselors. Some see counseling as a highly complex procedure, but more recent writers have simplified the process considerably. Egan,[3] for example, lists four stages: attending to the counselee and building rapport; responding to the counselee and helping him to explore his feelings, experiences, and behavior; building understanding in both counselor and counselee; and stimulating action which subsequently is evaluated by counselor and counselee together.

A psychologist named Lawrence Brammer has a longer but similar list: opening the interview and stating the problem(s); clarifying the problem and goals for counseling; structuring the counseling relationship and procedures; building a deeper relationship; exploring feelings, behavior, or thoughts; deciding on some plans of action, trying these out, and evaluating them; and terminating the relationship.[4]

To a large extent what we do in counseling will depend on the type of problem involved, the personalities of the helper and helpee, and the nature of their relationship. Building on the suggestions of Egan and Brammer, I would suggest that the counseling process has at least five steps, all of which are clearly illustrated in the Bible.

    a. *Building a relationship* between helper and helpee (John 6:63; 16:7-13; 1 John 4:6).

    b. *Exploring the problems*, trying to clarify issues and determine what has been done in the past to tackle the problem (Rom. 8:26).

    c. *Deciding on a course of action.* There may be several possible alternatives which could be tried one at a time (John 14:26; 1 Cor. 2:13).

    d. *Stimulating action* which helper and helpee evaluate together. When something doesn't work, try again (John 16:13; Acts 10:19, 20; 16:6).

    e. *Terminating the counseling relationship* and encouraging the helpee to apply what he has learned as he launches out on his own (Rom. 8:14).

Much of this is beautifully illustrated by Jesus on the road to Emmaus.

When He met the two men, Jesus used a variety of techniques to help them through their crisis and period of discouragement. Notice that this counseling situation did not take place in an office: there was no 50-minute hour, or Ph.D. diploma on the wall, or high fee; Jesus' counseling took place on a dusty road as the three of them walked along.

In Luke 24 we see that *Jesus first came alongside* the men and began traveling with them. Here was rapport-building—a showing of interest in their needs and a willingness to meet them where they were. Like Jesus, the helper must be willing to travel with his helpees if there is to be real therapeutic effectiveness. A cool aloofness rarely leads to successful counseling.

As they walked *Jesus began asking some very non-directive questions*: "What are you talking about?" He asked. As He began to explore the problem with them they responded with a question to Him.

"Are You the only one visiting Jerusalem and unaware of the things which have happened here these days?"

Jesus' reply is a classical client-centered response. "Which things?" He asked, and the men began talking.

As they traveled along, *Jesus spent a lot of time listening*. He surely didn't agree with what the men were saying, but He listened, gave them opportunity to express their frustrations, and showed them the love which sent Him to die for sinners in the first place.

After a period of time, *Jesus confronted* these men with their logical misunderstandings and failure to understand the Scriptures. The confrontation was gentle but firm, and it must have begun the process of stimulating the men to change their thinking and behavior. Then *Jesus began to teach* them, explaining the things from the Bible that concerned their problem. Today, centuries later, counseling most often casts the counselor into the role of a teacher who helps his counselees to learn where they have been in error and how they might think or behave more efficiently.

At the end of the journey, *Jesus got close* by accepting an invitation from the two men to eat a meal together. In any counseling situation it is important to get near to the counselee emotionally and psychologically, keeping in mind all of the ethical problems that this might involve.

Then an interesting thing happened. It is something that every helper dreams of doing with some of his helpees—especially the more difficult ones. Jesus "vanished from their sight!" In so doing *Jesus left them on their own and spurred them on to action*. This is the ultimate goal of all helping—to move the helpee to a point of independence where there is no longer any need to rely on help from the helper.

In other situations Jesus used different helping techniques. With Nicodemus He carried on a rational debate about apologetics. He encouraged and supported the timid woman with the issue of blood, confronted the woman at the well with her immorality, directed the woman taken in adultery to sin no more, criticized the proud Pharisees in a very directive fashion, prepared His disciples for the future when He sent them out two by two, and at all times was a model of how one ought to live the Christian life.

Following in His steps, the Christian counselor must live a life which is in close fellowship with God, shunning sin in his daily life and confessing sin when it occurs. We must meet people where they are, accept them as individuals to be loved even if their behavior is sinful and unlovely, seek at all times to be a model of what God wants us to be, and use every technique which is consistent with Scripture and which will bring behavior, thinking, and feeling into greater conformity with the Word of God.

A word of caution is essential at this point. In each of the approaches described above, including the counseling by Jesus on the road to Emmaus, there is a lengthy period of listening and rapport-building. Beginning counselors are often too anxious to come up with answers or to push the helpee to action. There needs to be a long period of understanding and exploration before we start jumping to solutions.

People Helping Principle 6

The ultimate goal of helping is to make disciples and disciplers of our helpees. This statement could be greatly misunderstood. It seems to imply that counseling is concerned only with spiritual matters or that the most important goal is to "get people saved" rather than to help them with their problems.

To clarify this sixth principle let us think for a moment of the Christian physician. Like every other believer, he too has a responsibility to be making disciples, but in the emergency room he does not pull out his Bible and start preaching. He starts with people where they are hurting. He demonstrates the love of Christ through his actions and concerns, realizing that the alleviation of suffering is honoring to Christ and is often a step towards evangelism (Prov. 14:31; Matt. 10:42). The physician does not avoid talk about spiritual matters, but this is not the major part of his treatment.

In the discipling process there are at least five steps. We must make contact, witness verbally, bring persons to the point of conversion, help them to grow as disciples, and teach them to disciple others. Much has been written about evangelism and witnessing, but only recently have we seen an emphasis on disciple-building.[5] The helper is concerned with both, but several conclusions are important.

a) The helper may come into a life at any point in these five steps. He may deal with a nonbeliever who has never heard the gospel, or he may counsel with a mature saint who has been growing as a disciple and discipler for many years. Where do we get the idea that counseling must be restricted to believers? "While we have opportunity," the Scriptures state, "let us do good to all men, and especially to those who are of the household of faith" (Gal. 6:10).

b) The helper may take his helpee through all five stages or he may be with him for a short time, making a few influences in his life and then moving out while someone else takes over. Sometimes one person makes contact and even does some counseling, another person witnesses, someone else leads the person to Christ, and then the discipling is taken over by still other people. Each of our lives is touched by a host of other lives. As helpers we need not be possessive of our helpees, assuming that we alone can help.

c) The spiritual can be introduced too quickly and too abruptly. Some helpees have been turned off in the past by well-meaning but pushy Christians who have rushed in to present the gospel or to give mini-sermons on how to live better lives. The helper must be sensitive to the Holy Spirit's leading, at times not even mentioning spiritual things at all. Sometimes a low-key approach to discipleship is the best way to begin.

d) Helping, like discipleship, involves the whole body of Christ. In Romans 12, 1 Corinthians 12, and elsewhere in Scripture we read that the body exists for mutual support, help, burden-bearing, and edification. We have settled too quickly into the idea of a one-to-one type of counseling. The church must be a healing community which supports the work of individual helpers and the growth of helpees.[6]

e) Discipleship counseling is concerned about the whole person. Man is a unity who rarely has a strictly spiritual need, a solely psychological abnormality, an exclusively social conflict, or a purely physical illness. When something goes wrong with one aspect of the unified person, the individual's whole being is affected. A healer may specialize in medicine, psychotherapy, or spiritual counseling, but each must remember that there is no sharp line between the spiritual, emotional, volitional, or physical in man. One symptom may cry for healing, but at such a time the entire body is off-balance. We must not deal with the spiritual and forget the person's psychological or physical needs; they go together, and the helper who forgets this does his helpee and his Lord a disservice.

These, then, are the principles of discipleship counseling. They concern the importance of the helper, the attitude of the helpee, the helping relationship, the importance of feeling, thinking, and actions, the use of helping skills, and the goal of discipleship. We turn now to some of the ways in which this approach can work out in practice.

4

FRIEND-TO-FRIEND HELPING

If you had a problem and needed help, to whom would you go? Think of someone by name.

The chances are very good that you would choose someone who is a friend, relative, or other close associate. There are not enough professional counselors to meet the needs of everyone in the community, and even if such help were available, many people would avoid it.

There are a number of reasons for this. The professional counselor is expensive, whereas counseling from a friend costs nothing. The professional is less available because of his office hours and answering service; the peer counselor may live next door or be as near as a telephone. To see a professional involves a certain stigma which the peer counselor does not have. "If I have to see a psychiatrist," many people reason, "I must really be in trouble."

To talk over the back fence to a neighbor is much less threatening. Furthermore, many people are afraid of professionals, viewing them as "mind-readers" or "head-shrinkers," but we usually don't think of nonprofessional counselors in this way. To consult a friend may have risks, especially if we feel uncomfortable about sharing intimate details of our lives, but to share with some stranger whom we have never met can be even more traumatic. I recall very vividly a lady who came to my office and announced that she had not slept for three nights because of her worry over our interview together. Such anxiety presents the professional with a rapport-building problem which the nonprofessional almost never encounters.

If it is true that many, even most, people in need turn to

a friend for help, then more attention needs to be given to peer counseling—especially Christian peer counseling. Church laymen already are doing significant amounts of counseling in their churches and communities. If these peer counselors (or "paraprofessionals," to use a more technical term) can recognize their limitations, they can with very little training make a significant impact on the mental health of people around them. This is real people helping.

In our discussion of peer counseling, let us look at five very important questions: Does friend-to-friend counseling work? Is counseling a gift that some people have to a special degree or is it something that everyone can do? How can peer counselors be made more effective? What are the peer counselor's goals? What are the dangers in peer counseling? These are questions which everyone who counsels should consider seriously.

DOES FRIEND-TO-FRIEND COUNSELING WORK?

Several years ago, a psychologist named Robert Carkhuff did a careful survey of all the research that had studied the effectiveness of what he called "lay helpers."[1] The conclusions of this psychological survey were startling. When lay counselors, with or without training, were compared with professionals it was discovered that "the patients of lay counselors do as well as or better than the patients of professional counselors."[2] This was true whether the peer counselors were working with normal adults having problems in getting along together, with children, with outpatients of psychiatric clinics, or with severely disturbed patients in psychiatric hospitals. Clearly there is strong evidence to support the conclusion that peer counselors are effective—sometimes even more so than highly trained professionals.

A number of reasons have been suggested for this finding. In contrast to professionals, the peer helper (a) is closer to the helpee, knows him as a friend, and is thus better able to understand his problem and to pick up non-verbal clues or to demonstrate a sincere empathy; (b) is more often available and is thus able to provide help consistently and whenever it is especially needed; (c) often knows about the helpee's family, work situation, life-style, beliefs, or neighborhood and can therefore take a more active part in guiding decisions or helping the helpee to change his life situation; (d) is able to communicate in language—including slang or one's native tongue—which the helpee can easily understand; and (e) is more down-to-earth, relaxed, open, informal, and inclined to introduce a tension-relieving humor. Very often the professional counselor is trying to work in accordance with some highly elaborate counseling theory. He is concerned about using proper technique, maintaining a professional image, and succeeding in his vocation. The peer helper couldn't care less about any of these. He knows nothing about theory, isn't trying to build a reputation as a counselor, and has no concerns about getting paid. Since he is primarily concerned about helping another human being, all of his efforts are directed toward that end, and he often ends up doing a better job that his highly trained professional counterpart.

IS FRIEND-TO-FRIEND COUNSELING A GIFT?

Very often I hear of students and other people who have no training in counseling but who discover that other people keep coming to them for help. Their telephones seem to be always ringing—sometimes to the consternation of their families—or people drop by their homes or dormitory rooms at all hours of the day or night to chat about personal needs. Why is it that some people appear to be "natural-born" counselors while others have no interest or seeming ability in this area at all? Might it be that some people are especially gifted or have innate abilities in the area of counseling?

Every Christian Should Be a People Helper

According to the Bible, every Christian should have a practical and sacrificial concern for the needs of his or her fellow human beings. James reminds us repeatedly that our faith is dead if it does not show itself in a practical concern for others (James 2:14-20). This same idea is emphasized elsewhere in the Scriptures. We must all be concerned about the interests of others (Phil. 2:4). We are all instructed to rejoice with people who rejoice and to weep in supportive empathy with those who weep (Rom. 12:15). We are all told to build up one another, to admonish one another, to encourage the fainthearted, to help the weak, and to be patient with the people around us (1 Thes. 5:11, 14). All spiritual men and women have a responsibility to gently heal or restore those who have fallen into sin, and we must all be involved in bearing one another's burdens (Gal. 6:1, 2). Whenever the opportunity arises, we must "do good to all men," and especially to those who are fellow believers (Gal. 6:10). Clearly, then, every Christian must reach out in love to other people, and counseling is one way in which we reach out. When family members, neighbors, fellow employees, or church members chat with us about some event in their lives or some problem issue, we who are motivated by Christian love will find ourselves counseling, whether we recognize it or not, and whether or not it is something we seek.

A Special Gift for People Helpers

While every Christian has a responsibility to help and counsel others, it is probable that counseling is one of the spiritual gifts which is given for the building up of the church and for the strengthening of individual believers. In his book *Love Therapy*, Paul Morris suggests that it is wrong to conclude that all Christians

> given proper understanding of the Scripture, are competent to counsel. . . . That counseling is one of the eighteen or so "spiritual gifts" is to me not a debatable

matter. And God has not given every believer this gift any more than he has given each believer the gift of "tongues" or of "pastor-teacher."

I know people who have never been to seminary and yet possess this gift. I wouldn't be afraid to trust these people with my mother or even the worst "incurable" psychotic. These are the most competent counselors in the world . . . . These men and women have been given *supernatural ability* by God, which they did not possess before he gave it.

Having said this, I want to say that the gift of counseling is not confined to relatively few people. It is widespread . . . . Training in the Scripture and in the science of applied psychology greatly enhances the effectiveness of someone with this gift. The more a person knows, the more that gift can be used.[3]

From this it should not be concluded that only the specially gifted are to be involved in counseling. In this respect, people helping is similar to evangelism or teaching. Although some believers have a special gift of evangelism (Eph. 4:11), every Christian is to be a witness, seeking to win men and women to Christ. Some Christians are specially gifted as teachers (Rom. 12:7 and Eph. 4:11), but all of us have responsibility for teaching our children and others. In the same way we must all be burden bearers and people helpers, even though some may have a special gift of counseling.

Morris suggests that people who possess this gift will have a strong desire to get involved in helping other people with their problems, will find that their counseling efforts often bring positive, constructive results, and will be concerned that their counseling gift is used for the edification or building up of the church. It is possible, in addition, that these are the very people who find themselves being approached frequently by those with counseling needs.

In Romans 12:8 we read about the gift of exhortation. The Greek word here is *paraklesis*, which means "coming alongside to help." The word implies such activities as admonishing, comforting, supporting, and encouraging people to face the future. All of this sounds very much like counseling, and it all refers to a gift given by God to a select group of believers.

Every Christian counselor, whether professional or paraprofessional, is the Holy Spirit's instrument. It is He alone who helps people, though He often does this through us (John 14:16, 26). Undoubtedly the Holy Spirit uses all believers in this task, but those with the gift of counseling are His special instruments for helping people in time of need.

HOW ARE PEER COUNSELORS TRAINED?

When Robert Carkhuff was doing his survey of peer and professional counselors, he decided to take a careful look at how counselors were being trained. Once again his findings were startling. At the beginning of his training the professional does a better job in helping people than does the layman. As training continues, however, the professional becomes less and less effective, so that he often ends up doing a worse job than the untrained lay counselor.[4]

Based on this evidence one might conclude that the peer counselor shouldn't get any training at all—especially if it comes from a professional. Might it be that training spoils our effectiveness as counselors? At one time in his career Paul Tournier wondered if he should become a psychiatrist, but his friends in psychiatry discouraged this. "Don't become one of us," they warned. "Such training will stifle you and take away your warmth and spontaneity."

The problem, however, is not so much whether or not a peer counselor should get training. The real issue concerns the *kind* of training that one gets. Professional training programs frequently focus on sophisticated research methods, complex personality theories, and complicated analyses of case histories. All of this pulls the trainee away from people and teaches him that knowledge of techniques or conformity to some counseling theory is of greater importance than rubbing elbows with people who are hurting.

In contrast, the nonprofessional is often less intellectual than the professional, less concerned about making the right diagnosis or using the best technique, and not at all interested in theory or research. He wants to help people and is often unwilling to sit through a long, complicated training program. The training that he gets, therefore, is usually brief but intensely practical and is geared toward developing empathy, warmth, genuineness, and the other traits that lead to effective counseling. Training for peer counselors (and probably for professionals) should be down-to-earth and practical, dealing with the real problems that real people have in their lives. While professionals can contribute a great deal to the training process, it is likely that other peer counselors and even our helpees also help us to learn.[5]

A number of different approaches have been developed for training peer counselors,[6] but some aspects of this training are common to almost all approaches. These training techniques are important not only to the peer counselors themselves but to those who are interested in helping others to in turn become peer counselors.

Select Carefully

It is important to *select trainees carefully*. There is probably some truth in the old idea that people who go into counseling often do so to solve their own problems. We might think that we *really* want to help others with our counseling, to alleviate suffering, or to make better disciples of Jesus Christ, but there might be other motives—the need to feel important, the desire for power over others, or the opportunity to talk openly to our counselees about sex. According to one writer, "solving problems in others which one cannot solve in oneself and taking the role of authority and helper to the troubled is a common way of escape from personal difficulties. Moreover, the drive to penetrate other people's lives . . . sometimes has its source in deep personal dissatisfaction."[7]

It is easy to get emotionally involved with the problems of others, so much so that the helper cannot remain objective or handle the tension. He then begins to develop unhealthy behavior in himself and may even urge others to engage in self-defeating behavior, which may then complicate the original problem. I suspect that professionals face these same dangers but that their training helps them to remain more objective and less inclined to use counseling sessions to solve their own problems—more willing to check their behavior and counseling motives against the objective opinion of supervisors or other counselors. The place to avoid some of these problems, however, is right at the beginning. The prospective helper should carefully and honestly examine his or her motives for wanting to do counseling, and the trainer should do likewise.

Focus on the Person

Effective training will *focus on the prospective counselor as a person*. If "in any helping relationship, the personality, values, attitudes, and beliefs of the helper are of primary importance," then these should be of primary importance in a training program. The helper's strong and weak points should be considered. If you want to help people by counseling, you should examine yourself in the light of Scripture (Psa. 119:9-11; 139:23, 24) and seek with God's help to make appropriate changes in your life. You should look at your special abilities and gifts, and you should be honest enough to talk about yourself to others. No person, it has been suggested, "can come to know himself except as an outcome of disclosing himself to another."[8] This self-disclosure must be to fellow human beings and to God (James 5:16).

As the peer counselor begins his or her work there will

often be a need for encouragement and psychological support, especially when the counseling gets difficult. The beginner (and the "pro" as well) may often feel a need to discuss his or her insecurities as a helper, or there might be a need to talk about the anxieties and temptations that can come when we are closely involved with the intimate details of another person's life. Beginning counselors should find a way to talk over these issues with someone who is a more experienced helper.

Learn Skills

Proper taining of helpers involves *learning of skills*. This means having some knowledge of what to do, though knowledge alone is not enough. Effective learning of skills involves understanding what is to be done, watching others as they demonstrate the skills, and then practicing the skills.[9] Knowing, watching, and doing are therefore all-important in training counselors.

Provide Experience

Effective training *must be combined with on-the-job experience*. This makes the professional feel a little uncomfortable because it seems to suggest that novice counselors should be turned loose on unsuspecting troubled people to solve their problems by "playing psychiatrist." It must be remembered, however, that laymen are *already* counseling real people, so our task is to help them do better what they are *already doing*. The idea that long periods of training must precede practice is crumbling in many kinds of professional training programs. Medical students and nurses, for example, go on to the wards very early in their training. We get new converts involved in witnessing soon after their conversion. The same on-the-job training, accompanied by training, is likely to characterize future peer counselor training as well.

Recognize Limitations

Finally, we must teach peer counselors *when and how to make referrals*, and we must show that there can be *no cookbook answers*. Every counselor would like to have a cookbook—a "how to do it" manual that would always be at our fingertips to give us six or eight principles for handling every problem of life. Such manuals do not exist, and if they did they wouldn't be able to describe human behavior in all its complexity. When the beginning counselor finds a formula which reduces all problems and their solutions to a few steps, he first gets excited, but this is followed quickly by skepticism. Beginners often think they can learn to counsel perfectly, and if they fail they blame their training or their own failure to comprehend. It is better to recognize that God made each person unique. Each problem is also unique, requiring a unique approach, and sometimes we aren't successful in our people-helping efforts. At such times referral to another counselor may be our best alternative. This will be discussed further in Chapter 7.

WHAT ARE THE PEER COUNSELOR'S GOALS?

There has been much debate in the psychological journals about what the peer counselor is able to do properly. Some professionals have taken the view that laymen should restrict themselves to simple tasks—like answering the telephone, scoring tests, or giving encouragement—until the professional can come along with his or her expertise to do the psychotherapy. This is an untenable, perhaps even cocky, position to hold in view of the demonstrated effectiveness of peer counselors.

It is probable that peer counselors, like professionals, can do any or all of the following:

—give support in times of need;
—encourage expression of emotion;
—help counselees to get intellectual insight into their problem behavior;

—confront counselees with sin, irresponsibility, self-defeating behavior, or inconsistencies in their lives;

—teach social skills;

—encourage and guide counselees as they try new ways of coping with problems, making decisions, or struggling to avoid falling into sin;

—help people to find and use information;

—work to eliminate undesirable behavior;

—help those who are searching for meaning or purpose in life;

—guide those who have theological problems and are seeking answers;

—challenge counselees with the need to commit their lives to Christ and to grow as disciples;

—refer counselees when professional or other help is necessary.

This is not meant to be an exhaustive list, nor is it meant to hide the fact that professional assistance will sometimes be necessary. If, for example, the helpee is considering suicide, sees visions or hears strange noises, threatens himself or others, is severely depressed, or talks and acts in a bizarre manner, then the professional counselor's training and expertise with these severe problems makes referral a necessity. In addition, there may be times when someone has difficult theological questions, complains of physical symptoms, needs help with financial planning, or is in legal difficulty. These are all situations which are beyond the experience and knowledge of most peer helpers. Referral to a pastor, doctor, banker, lawyer, or other expert is the best way to handle these situations, but one should always remember that referral is *not* an admission of failure. It can be a significant step in helping people with their problems.

Alcoholics Anonymous (AA) has shown conclusively that friends can be effective in helping their peers, even in serious problems. The AA movement has even raised the idea that people with problems of their own can at times become very good counselors. Perhaps few would agree with the writer who suggested that "the best way to treat a person is to get him to treat someone else,"[10] but peer counselors *can* provide help in a variety of situations. To ignore peer counselors or to confine them to menial counseling tasks is to ignore a huge resource for helping people in trouble.

WHAT ARE THE DANGERS OF
FRIEND-TO-FRIEND COUNSELING?

In everyday conversation there are some things that are too personal to talk about. We rarely ask other people about their finances, for example, or their sex life, their anxieties, or the status of their marriage. In a helping relationship, however, these topics are often discussed openly because they may be the very issues that are bothering the person who needs help.

Counselor Curiosity

This freedom to talk freely can raise some ethical issues which the peer helper will be wise to heed. First is the issue of *counselor curiosity*. Sometimes in our counseling we temporarily forget the helpee's needs and start asking for information which primarily satisfies our own curiosity. The helper must be alert to this tendency and seek to avoid it, especially when the topic of conversation deals with issues that border on gossip or on the details of the helpee's sexual behavior.

Sexual Stimulation

Closely connected with this is the issue of *sexual stimulation*. This can go both ways (from helper to helpee and vice-versa), and sometimes we stimulate the other person without intending to do so or without either of us being aware of what is happening. The male counselor who puts his arm around the counselee to give comfort may not realize that his female or male counselee might misinterpret the meaning of the hug. A modest amount of physical contact between helper and helpee is not necessarily wrong, since it can at times be very supportive and encouraging. But we must be careful to ask "how does the helpee interpret this?" and "what satisfaction is this contact giving me?" It is absolutely crucial that the Christian helper avoid all appearance of evil. By forgetting this principle some counselors—including pastoral counselors—have become overly involved with their helpees and as a result have ruined their family, lives, and ministry. To say "But it would never happen to me" is to already be walking on dangerous ground (1 Cor. 10:12).

Confidence Leaks

Confidence leaks are a third danger for the peer helper. It is true that the peer helper is not legally bound by the same confidentiality code that is so important to professionals. But if the peer counselor talks about his or her counselees, this borders on gossip. Even when we try to hide the details of the case, it is likely that somebody in the neighborhood or church will guess who is being talked about. Such talk should be avoided. It does nothing for our spiritual well-being and may very well shake the helpee's faith in the helper.

Spiritual Balance

Underemphasis or overemphasis on the spiritual can be another danger. In the case of underemphasis, the helpee is denied the resources of the Scriptures or prayer and sometimes never even hears the gospel because the helper is afraid to raise the issue. In the second place the helpee might be driven away—scared off by religion—or be led to believe that the spiritual part of our being is all that matters. Such a view has no support in Scripture, nor can we maintain that if we are right with the Lord all problems will vanish automatically. The spiritual must enter our counseling, since it is crucially important, but it should be used appropriately rather than overemphasized.

Avoiding the Dangers

How can we avoid these and other dangers? For one thing, we can develop a spiritual protection. Daily study of the Scriptures and an active prayer life, even during the counseling session, can keep our minds from wandering and our mouths from saying something harmful or even sinful. Second, it helps when we are alert to the dangers. To be forewarned is to be forearmed! Third, we can deliberately seek to avoid compromising situations, overemphasis on sexually arousing topics, and other dangers. Finally, we can get into the habit of discussing our counseling in confidence with some other person—a pastor, a professional counselor, or simply a friend who can help us keep things in perspective and free from danger.

The Worst Danger of All

The training and use of peer counselors to help each other is an exciting concept which, until recently, has almost been ignored by the church. We train church people to witness. We teach them how to teach others, and now we are even training them how to disciple others. Perhaps as a part of this we should be training them how to *relate to* others—to bear one another's burdens and to counsel with each other.

There are dangers in friend-to-friend helping, but there can also be tremendous benefits, especially when the peer counselors have had some practical training. It is true, of course, that a little knowledge about counseling can be a dangerous thing, but no knowledge and training can be even worse. And to have no concern about helping others on a peer-to-peer level may be the worst danger of all.

5

HELPING IN A CRISIS

As we go through life, all of us at times encounter crises. The death of a loved one, the birth of a deformed child, the breakdown in a marriage, the failure to be accepted into college, the occurrence of an automobile accident—all these are among those events of life that shake us and can make us feel threatened, anxious, confused, and depressed.

Stated somewhat formally, a crisis is any event or series of circumstances which threatens a person's well-being and interferes with his routine of daily living.

Most of us move along from day to day, meeting the problems and challenges of life in a more or less efficient manner. Periodically, however, a situation arises which is so novel and threatening that our usual ways of handling problems no longer work. Suddenly we are forced to rely on new and untried methods to deal with the tension that has come into our lives.

In the past people usually turned to relatives on such occasions, seeking their advice and accepting their help and sympathy. In many parts of the world this still takes place, but in North America things are different. We are a mobile people who move frequently and are often far away from family members who could give the greatest support in times of crisis. In the absence of relatives, therefore, we turn to neighbors, friends, fellow church members, and pastors. These are the people who are on the scene at the moment of crisis and are best able to help.

THE MAJOR KINDS OF CRISES

Crises can be divided into two broad categories.[1] Developmental crises are those which occur at predicted times as we journey through life. Facing the first day in school, coping with adolescence, adjusting to marriage, dealing with the insecurities of middle age, adapting to retirement—all of these are crisis situations which require extra effort on the part of an individual and his family. Such crises may be very severe, but they are usually predictable in advance and are resolved as the individual learns to adjust to a new stage in life.

Accidental crises, as the name implies, are much less predictable, and as a result they often hit with greater force. A sudden loss of status or possessions, the traffic death of a loved one, the unexpected ending of an engagement, the sudden loss of a job—any of these can put extreme demands on an individual and create confusion as he ponders what to do next.

REACTING TO CRISES

Usually the person under crisis turns first to his habitual ways of dealing with problems. Very soon, however, he discovers that the old coping devices don't work. The initial tension is still there, but in addition the person feels a sense of frustration and confusion because of his inability to cope. At this point all of one's inner resources are mobilized. The person tries a number of trial-and-error methods to deal with the problem, he draws on his reserves of physical strength, he racks his brain to think of creative new ways for dealing with the situation, and he learns to accept or make the best of circumstances which cannot be changed. If all of this fails and the problem continues, the person eventually collapses, either physically or mentally or both.[2] Very often this is what happens in a so-called nervous breakdown. There are no more resources or stamina left for coping with the stress. The person gives up exhausted, withdraws into a world of unreality, or persists irrationally in some behavior which may deny the problem but does nothing to solve it.

THE UNIQUENESS OF EACH CRISIS

Every crisis situation is unique. The circumstances, personalities, and psychological makeup of the people involved; one's past experience (or lack of it) in handling crises; the availability of others who can help—all of these influence what happens in a given crisis situation. It is difficult to predict what any individual, including ourselves, might do in a crisis. Some people collapse almost immediately, while others discover that they have tremendous inner reserves which enable them to cope with even prolonged periods of intense crisis.

Some characteristics, however, seem to be very common.[3] There is, for example, *anxiety*, which sometimes causes the person to make a poor judgment, which then adds to the problems. Often there is a sense of *helplessness*. The person doesn't know what to do and often feels ashamed because he cannot be more self-reliant. A *dependence on others* is often inevitable, but this can also create problems. Sometimes the person feels guilty for being so dependent, frustrated with his inability to make decisions, and angry because other people are running his life. This all contributes to a *loss of self-esteem* because the person feels vulnerable and not in control. *Anger* over the whole situation is a common emotion which is sometimes hidden but often directed to others—including the people who are trying to help. In his frustration the person in a crisis doesn't know who to be mad at, so he lashes out against those who are closest and most likely to stick with him in spite of the anger. Sometimes there is anger at God followed by feelings of guilt. Often there is also a *decreasing efficiency* in our daily behavior. Ruminating on the problem, worrying about what will happen next, questioning why it happened in the first place—these all take time, energy, and attention which normally would be directed to other activities.

COPING IN A CRISIS

In many respects a crisis is more than an increase in tension or an upset in our daily pattern of living. A crisis represents a turning point which has a bearing on one's future adjustment and mental health. If we are able to cope with the crisis, to adapt to our new circumstances, or to find efficient ways for solving the crisis problem, then we have developed a greater self-confidence and experience, which will help us deal more effectively with future crises. If, on the other hand, a person is unable to cope, there are feelings of failure or incompetence which spill over to the next crisis and make it even harder to adapt in the future.

According to one psychiatrist,[4] it is common in crises for a person to both mobilize his own inner resources and to seek help from the people around him. Others see these signs of increasing tension and are stimulated to come to the distressed person's assistance. Professional counselors can help here, but the best helpers are those whom the person in crisis already knows, respects, and loves. The closer we are to the person in crisis—the more we are aware of the situation—the more likely we are to be called on and the easier it is for us to intervene on our own initiative. It is clear, therefore, that the family and the church are of crucial importance in crisis counseling. How an individual relates to those around him will determine to a considerable degree how successful he will be in finding a solution which, in turn, will promote or hamper his future mental health.

How then can we help a person in a time of crisis? To begin we might examine Table 2. This shows some unhealthy and healthy ways of dealing with a crisis. When sickness, death in the family, financial losses, marital strife, and other crises come along, the counselor's goal is to help the person to avoid unhealthy behaviors, feelings, or

TABLE 2*

*Healthy and Unhealthy Ways
to Meet A Crisis*

Unhealthy Ways to Meet a Crisis

1. Deny that a problem exists.
2. Evade the problem (via alcohol, for example).
3. Refuse to seek help or to accept it.
4. Hide the fact that you have feelings of sorrow, anger, guilt, etc.
5. Don't think through the nature of the crisis situation.
6. Give no thought to practical ways in which you might deal with the crisis.
7. Blame others for causing the crisis and expect that somebody else is totally responsible for curing it.
8. Turn away from friends or family.
9. Refuse to pray about the crisis.
10. Convince yourself that a crisis is evidence of God's punishment or disfavor.

Healthy Ways to Meet a Crisis

1. Face the fact that there is a problem.
2. Attempt to understand the situation more fully.
3. Open channels of communication with friends, relatives, pastors, or others who might be able to help you.
4. Face up to your negative feelings of guilt, anxiety, or resentment, and consider actions and alternative ways of viewing the situation so that you can deal with these feelings.
5. Separate the changeable from the unchangeable in the situation and accept that which cannot be changed.
6. Explore practical ways of coping with the problem, and take steps (however small) in handling the problem in a practical way.
7. Accept responsibility for coping with problems, even problems which seem to have arisen from situations beyond your control.
8. Draw closer to friends and family, especially those who are helpful.
9. Pray about the matter, honestly sharing your concerns with God.
10. Do not forget the sovereignty of God, who loves mankind and is both aware of our crises and concerned about us.

*Adapted with permission from H. J. Clinebell, Jr., *Basic Types of Pastoral Counseling* (Nashville: Abingdon Press, 1966), pp. 163-4.

thoughts and to focus instead on that which is healthy and constructive.

To do this the crisis counselor must be geographically near the person in crisis (it is difficult to help someone across the country), immediately available (even if this means in the middle of the night), mobile (so that we can go to the person in need, especially when he or she cannot come to us), and flexible in counseling methods.[5] Professional counselors who maintain rigid office hours often fail to meet these criteria and are thus less effective in crisis situations than are family members, friends, neighbors, church members, and ministers. The latter can be especially helpful in times of crisis because they symbolize hope and theological stability to a person in the midst of discouragement and great uncertainty.

CRISIS INTERVENTION

There can be no standard formula or cookbook approach for helping a person in crisis. There are some things, however, which can be done in almost every case.

Make Contact

It is difficult to be very effective in crisis counseling if the helper is half a country (or even half a block) away from the helpee. As Christians we believe that we can intervene from afar through prayer, and this must not be overlooked, but whenever possible we should also show personal concern by our presence, warmth, and willingness to listen. The sooner we can be there, the more likely we are to help.

Reduce Anxiety

Contrary to some popular beliefs, this is not done by encouraging the helper to think about something else. To take an extreme example, if at a funeral home we find ourselves talking to a surviving mate about baseball or the stock market, we may be avoiding the reality of death in order to reduce our own anxiety. But this doesn't work very well with people who are in crises. They often want to talk about the situation, describe what happened, think back to happier times before the crisis, and feel free to express their emotions of sadness, grief, remorse, or anger.

At such times the helper can demonstrate calmness, concern, and acceptance. He can bring the comfort of the Scriptures and pray with the helpee, making sure, however, that these are not gimmicks to keep everyone from talking about the hurt and expressing feelings.

If the helper doesn't know much about the situation, he or she will want to find out, if possible, when the crisis started and what went on before it began. In so doing we can sometimes spot the source of the trouble and begin to deal with it. If a person says, for example, "everything was going great for me until I started college," we might be able to assume that there is something in the college setting that is causing the crisis symptoms.

Sometimes anxiety-reduction will involve bearing the brunt of the helpee's anger, helping him to see his problem, commending him for steps already taken to face the crisis, and helping him to see that all is not hopeless. This, of course, can backfire if done improperly. Romans 8:28, for example, can be stated in a glib fashion which angers the helpee, especially if he feels that the verse-quoter has not taken the time to really understand the situation.

When several people are involved in a crisis, it helps if you can deal with the most anxious person first and send away the curious onlookers. Several years ago our family saw a little boy get hit by a car. As my wife, who is a nurse, applied first aid and talked calmly to the distressed mother, an older brother appeared on the scene. In an agitated manner he yelled, "Mommy, is Jimmy going to die?" Immediately the whole scene got tense until my wife assured the older brother that Jimmy would probably be okay and then suggested that the mother might want a coat or sweater over her shoulders as she rode in the ambulance.

The older brother ran off to get the sweater and the situation calmed down considerably.

Focus on the Issues

In the midst of a crisis it is easy to see a mass of issues all of which seem to be overwhelming. The helper can do several things at this point. First, he or she can help the person in crisis to explore the present situation by describing his feelings, thoughts, and plans (if he has any), his view of the events that have taken place, and his efforts to solve the problem. This is a process of sorting out the problems one at a time, finding out what is threatening and seeing what has been done or might be done about the situation.

At some time there needs to be a narrowing down of what the real problems are, an inventory of the person's resources (what money, ability, people, and opportunities are available), a listing of the different alternatives that the person has before him, and an evaluation of each of these. If the helpee has not raised all of the alternatives, raise a few yourself. For each alternative, try to decide with the helpee what is feasible, what will really help with the problem, and what is easiest to accomplish.

Shortly before writing this chapter I visited the tornado area of a city in which a number of homes had been damaged. One house was completely destroyed except for one wall, which was still standing. Across the wallpaper, in bold black letters, someone had written "The Richardsons will build again!" Following the crisis their alternative had been decided!

Remember that people in crises are often very suggestable, so we must be careful not to push for our own solutions. We must also help people to be realistic and practical. The last thing a person in crisis needs is to add failure to his other problems. Indeed, the fear of further failure is what immobilizes many people in times of crisis, and they need help and encouragement in deciding to act.

In helping with a crisis the helper can do much to

mobilize church or community aid. Massive prayer support can not only sustain a person through a crisis, but it is also an encouraging demonstration that people really care. To this there sometimes can be added the more tangible help about which James writes: "If a brother or sister is without clothing and in need of daily food, and one of you says to them, 'Go in peace, be warmed and be filled,' and yet you do not give them what is necessary for their body, what use is that?" (James 2:15, 16). Faith in Jesus Christ, and commitment to Him, should at times manifest itself by helping people in a tangible way, with money, supplies, baby-sitting, helping around the house, or other down-to-earth assistance.

Encourage Action

Sometimes, with or without help, a person will decide on some course of action but will then be afraid to move ahead with the plan. Here is where a helper can encourage the helpee to acquire skills, if these are needed, and to stick with him as he takes action. One must be careful not to be doing things for the helpee all the time. It is easy for all of us to sit back, to "let somebody else do it," and then to complain about the quality of the service. The person in crisis needs to be helped to help himself. He needs to evaluate his actions with the counselor's help and, if necessary, to come up with different or better alternatives when an earlier plan is unsuccessful.

All of this assumes, of course, that the helper and helpee are the only ones involved in meeting the crisis situation. We should remember, however, that most crises begin with a series of environmental events or circumstances. Very often the most effective way to take action in a crisis is to change the environment. To help the counselee get another job, to mobilize the community to help rebuild a house or provide for medical expenses, to counsel with relatives or friends who may have been causing much of the stress in the first place—these are all ways in which we can reduce the force of the crisis by making an intervention in the environment.

Help with Acceptance

Paul Tournier suggests in one of his books that acceptance is the first step toward dealing with a serious problem. Sometimes a crisis will bring permanent change. The death of a loved one, the destruction of property, or the discovery of a terminal illness, for example, are all events which must be accepted and dealt with. To do otherwise is to deny the problem and to delay its solution until later.

Acceptance, like healing, takes time. Often it involves a painful, conscious thinking about the situation, an expressing of feelings, a readjustment of one's life-style, a building of new relationships, and a planning for the future. Acceptance may involve risks and potential failure. It is most successful when we are surrounded by sincere, patient, helpful friends, and when we know in a personal way the Savior who told us to come to Him with our burdens, to cast them on Him, and to experience the peace and guidance that give us real hope and stability during times of crisis (Matt. 11:28, 29; Psa. 55:22; 32:8). We should remember, however, that when a person casts his burden on the Lord, the Lord may sustain him through other human beings— like the writer or readers of this book.

JESUS AS A CRISIS COUNSELOR

A familiar example of crisis counseling is recorded in John 11. It involves a terminal illness, personal danger, and the loss of a loved one.

When Lazarus of Bethany became seriously ill, his sisters sent a message to Jesus: "Lord, behold, he whom You love is sick."

According to the Biblical account, Jesus loved Lazarus, Mary, and Martha. Perhaps more than anyplace else, their home near Jerusalem was a place where Jesus could relax. And yet, instead of hurrying to their need, he sat around for two days. Jesus, of course, knew what was going on in Bethany, and He even used the crisis to teach the disciples (vv. 4, 9-15) before they realized that Lazarus' illness was terminal.

The disciples, however, were facing a crisis of their own. Jesus' life was in danger, and so were theirs, because of their association with a wanted man (vv. 8, 16). To appear in public was to risk violent death, but when Jesus told them that Lazarus was dead they agreed to accompany the Lord to Bethany.

When they arrived, the scene was one of great sadness. A number of friends had come to comfort the sisters in their loss, but when Martha heard that Jesus was coming she left the house and went down the road to meet Him. Notice how Jesus handled the situation:

—He explained what was happening to the confused disciples (vv. 4, 14, 15).

—He let Martha express her feelings and confusion (vv. 21, 22).

—He reassured her in a calm manner and instilled hope (vv. 23, 25, 26).

—He pointed her to the Person of Christ (v. 25).

—He let Mary express her feelings, feelings which might have contained some anger (v. 32).

—He did not stop people from grieving but, on the contrary, expressed His own sorrow (vv. 33-36).

—He calmly bore the hostility of many of the saddened mourners (v. 37), even though it deeply moved Him(vv. 37, 38).

Then Jesus took action—action which changed the sadness into joy, brought glory to God, and caused many people to believe in Christ (vv. 38-45). On this occasion Jesus did not send the observers away, as He had at the raising of Jairus' daughter, but by calling Lazarus from the grave He demonstrated conclusively His victory over death, the greatest of all crises. A few days later, when he Himself was executed, Jesus approached the cross with calmness and then rose again. Little wonder that the Apostle Paul could shout to the Corinthians that death had been swallowed up in victory and that believers had certainty of a life after death, a life with Christ Himself (1 Cor. 15:51-58).

It is true that none of us can bring a dead person back to life, as Jesus did, but it is also true that as crisis helpers we can employ each of the other techniques that Jesus used during this crisis in Bethany. Even without the resurrection of Lazarus, the crisis in Bethany would have served a useful purpose. Jesus tried to convince the disciples of this (John 11:4), but they obviously didn't get the message until later.

CRISIS HELPING TODAY

The same is true of most crises today. They are painful, traumatic experiences, but they can also be growing experiences which provide good opportunity for learning. I remember the words of a friend who once remarked, "We never have problems around here—we just have opportunities!"

According to Dr. Gene W. Brockopp of the Suicide Prevention and Crisis Service in Buffalo, New York, crises can be both helpful and therapeutic.[6] They often throw a person into such a state of tension that there is a breakdown of defenses, a strong willingness to change, and an unusual openness to the suggestions of a counselor. If the helpee is able to mobilize his resources and solve his problems, there is an increase in his confidence and self-esteem. Sometimes crises teach the person to look more objectively at problems when they arise and to solve them more efficiently. All of this contributes to his mental well-being and psychological stability. It might be added that crises also have a way of alerting people to spiritual issues and teaching them to lean more fully on the Christ who called Lazarus out of the grave. Everyone doesn't react this way, of course. Some get critical and angry with God, but others look back to crises as a turning point in their spiritual development.

As we have seen, however, people in crises are often confused, suggestable, guilty, and self-condemning. Very

often they feel so hopeless about a situation that they contemplate suicide as one of their most viable alternatives. In
dealing with such people, it would be easy for a helper to
play on the person's guilt and manipulate him into making
some kind of spiritual decision which he may later regret,
resent, and repudiate.

THE SPIRITUAL IMPLICATIONS OF A CRISIS

When faced with the death of Lazarus and the dangers
to his own life, Jesus did not deny the spiritual implications
of what was happening. He used the situation to teach
spiritual truths, to show how to cope with crises, and to
demonstrate the power of God in the lives of His children.
Notice, however, that in pointing to the spiritual He did
not play on people's emotions, nor did He rob them of their
freedom to doubt (John 11:16), to criticize (v. 37), to resist
(vv. 46-53), or to turn to Him and believe (v. 45).

God uses crises to bring people to Himself. He uses
crises to help Christians grow and to mature as disciples.
Our task as people helpers is to be open to the leading of the
Holy Spirit, trusting that He will show us when and how to
bring spiritual issues into our crisis-helping in a way that
will draw the helpee closer to the Lord and ultimately bring
glory to God.

6

HELPING ON THE TELEPHONE

Counseling over the telephone is hardly a new idea. In our technological era we have come to realize that "help is as near as the telephone," and it is to the telephone that most people turn when they have a sick kid, a leaky faucet, a problem in making sense of an income tax form, or a more personal problem.

Several years ago church leaders began to realize the value of ministering to people through use of the telephone, and a number of "dial-for-help" counseling services were established, first in England and Australia, and later in North America. In 1958, when the Los Angeles Suicide Prevention Center was established, the founders turned to the telephone as an instrument through which people could be counseled. It has been estimated that there are now several hundred telephone counseling clinics in the United States alone.[1] These include pastoral-counseling, suicide-prevention, poison-control, teenage hotline, drug information, contact for the elderly, and a variety of other helpful services which the caller receives free via the telephone.

THE NEGLECTED METHOD

Telephone counseling is hardly ever mentioned in counseling books, even though this may be one of the most common types of people helping that is done. In the opinion of one writer, professionals "seem to have judged telephone counseling to be different from *real* therapy and, hence, did not perceive it as worthy of their attention. A common experience at telephone counseling services is for the professional staff to gradually detach themselves from counseling over the telephone in order to focus on face-to-face therapy, leaving the non-professionals to do the telephone counseling."[2]

As a result of this withdrawal by professionals, telephone counseling centers, for the most part, are staffed by peer volunteers—volunteers whose ability to help people by talking on the phone has been clearly demonstrated.[3] With some problems (suicide prevention, for example) the peer counselor is considered to be far more helpful than the professional whom he replaces. This has led one of the best-known leaders in suicide prevention to formulate what he has called "Letman's Law:"[4]

> The more severe and acute the suicidal crisis is, the *less* one needs to be professionally trained in order to manage it effectively.

Most of this "managing" takes place over the telephone. To be an effective people helper, therefore, the Christian leader and helper should have some understanding of telephone counseling and how it works.

THE UNIQUENESS OF TELEPHONE HELPING

Several years ago, during a lengthy visit to Switzerland, my family and I lived in a delightful chalet which did not have a telephone. This was a unique experience and one which was so relaxing that I tried—unsuccessfully—to talk my family into having our telephone removed when we got home. Some of the arguments I got in favor of the telephone were most convincing: it is a means of keeping in touch with friends and relatives, it is almost indispensable in emergencies when one needs help in a hurry, and it is convenient for getting information or making purchases. The worlds of business, education, and government would hardly survive without the telephone, and neither would most individuals—at least in America. It is surprising, therefore, that the counseling profession, which specializes in interpersonal communication, should for so long have ignored the unique features of telephone counseling. Stated briefly, telephone helping is (1) extremely convenient, (2) especially suited to emergencies, and (3) particularly valuable to certain kinds of people whose life-styles and problems prohibit them from getting face-to-face counseling help.[5]

THE CONVENIENCE OF TELEPHONE HELPING

Let's begin with the *conveniences* of telephone counseling.

Less Threatening

When talking on the telephone, the helpee often feels less threatened because he or she is more in control of the situation. It is he who makes the call in the first place, fully aware that if he doesn't like the helper's personality and questions or if he feels otherwise uncomfortable he can get out of the situation simply by hanging up. Often the helpee also feels more comfortable when he is talking from the safety and security of his own home rather than in an unfamiliar clinic office, church parsonage, or living room of a friend. For people who are afraid of being trapped by a counselor, a telephone is "the only way to go." It is a safe way to reach out for help.

Anonymity

A second convenience of the telephone is that it lets people remain anonymous. Some individuals are so threatened by face-to-face contact that they don't even want their names to be known. It is pretty difficult to remain anonymous when you are talking to someone in person (although this sometimes happens on planes, when people pour out their troubles to a seat-mate, secure in the knowledge that there probably will be no further contact after both passengers are swallowed up by the crowds and halls of the air terminal). When you use the telephone, however, especially if you call a telephone clinic and talk to a stranger, you can talk about the intimate details of your life without risking rejection by someone who knows your identity. Even when friends are talking, the telephone creates a safe distance. Back in my bachelor days I preferred calling for dates via the telephone because I knew it would be less embarrassing for me in case I got turned down.

Availability

Thirdly, there are times when telephone counseling is the only possibility available. The person who is ill and without transportation, for example, or the helpee who is many miles from a helper, may find that talking on the telephone is the most feasible way to get help. The college girl who calls her mother to talk about dating problems may be using the best means at her disposal. People also use the phone when it would be most inappropriate for a counselor to be present. A colleague of mine once received a call from a former student who had recently been married. The couple was having some difficulties in sexual adjustment during the first night of the honeymoon, so they decided to call their old psychology professor, long distance, at 2 A.M. The professor gave them some encouragement and instruction in a situation in which telephone counseling was undoubtedly the best approach to take!

Time-Saving

So far we have mentioned only the conveniences for the *helpee*, but of course telephone counseling also has advantages for the *helper*—especially when the helper is a non-professional who is not concerned about normal business requirements (scheduling, fees, etc.). Telephone counseling can often save the helper the time and inconvenience of setting up a counseling interview. He can use the telephone to "keep in touch" with his helpees by giving them a frequent call to maintain contact and show interest. At times when the helper is unable to meet with a helpee personally, a brief telephone conversation may be all that is needed. This is especially true during periods of crisis, when the helpee needs to know that someone cares, but when it is not practical to have daily interviews. The anonymous nature of telephone conversations can also be valuable to the speakers:

> The telephone therapist ... will be far more like the patient's ideal than the face-to-face therapist, since the patient is presented with only a part of the reality. On the telephone, we receive none of the visual clues about a person that we receive in face-to-face contact. We have no idea what the person we are talking with looks like, nor can we see facial expressions, and finally, we get none of the body language clues to his thoughts, feelings, and personality that we generally receive in a face-to-face contact.... The telephone contact, much more than the face-to-face interview, permits the patient to make of the therapist what he will ... [and] what he *needs*.[6]

EMERGENCIES AND TELEPHONE HELPING

Undoubtedly the time when telephone counseling is most helpful is during *emergencies*. By using the telephone, a caller can get help fast, without going through all the rigmarole of setting up an appointment, traveling to a meeting place or, in the case of professional clinics, filling out forms and having one's name put on a waiting list. A telephone call helps to bypass these barriers. It can often bring immediate help, even though this may consist only of making contact with someone who can instill hope and bring objectivity into a tense situation.

Many people have found that it is therapeutic just to have someone whom they can call should the need arise. The distraught teenager who knows that he can always call the church leader or the basketball coach, for example, may never actually make the call, but he feels better because of his assurance that he could get help quickly if he needed it.

Whether they are facing an emergency or not, some people benefit from telephone counseling because their personalities won't let them get any other kind of help. People who live alone, for example, are sometimes unable to cope with intimate, face-to-face contacts with other people, but they might be able to talk on the telephone. Likewise, the person who is desperate often finds that he is confused and overwhelmed by circumstances, but a telephone contact may be his lifeline to getting help. Highly insecure people also turn to the telephone. Adolescents, for example, sometimes have difficulty admitting their vulnerability and need for help, but a telephone contact, because it is less threatening, often directs them to the help they need.

LIMITATIONS OF TELEPHONE HELPING

In teaching counseling courses I place great emphasis on the fact that the counselor should watch the counselee as well as listen to what he says. We can learn a lot about a person just by looking at how he is dressed, how he cares for himself physically, how he walks, or how he sits in the chair. His facial expression, indications of tenseness, body movement, tears, or way of breathing can all be extremely important nonverbal clues which help us to understand him better and build rapport more quickly. In addition, by observing gestures, head nods, and eye movements, the helpee can get a pretty good indication of whether or not the helper is listening and trying to understand.

As soon as we start talking on the telephone all of these visual clues are gone, and this presents problems for everyone. Since he can't see the helper, the helpee doesn't know how his problems are being received. As we have already indicated, this is comforting to some helpees, especially if they are discussing embarrassing or sinful behavior. But it can also be comforting to know that the helper accepts you, is understanding, and is giving his undivided attention to what is being said. The telephone caller doesn't see this, so the counselor must demonstrate it verbally.

The telephone helper, however, is probably having a few problems of his own. Since he too is cut off from verbal clues, he must listen very carefully not only to what is being said but to such things as tone of voice, hesitations, changes in volume or speed or pitch, sighing, shakiness in the voice, or any other sounds which might reveal something about the helpee. If the caller is a stranger it might be difficult to tell either the sex or age of the person and, of course, we have no clues about his or her grooming or nonverbal nervous mannerisms. Sometimes, therefore, we have to ask what we need to know—how old a person is, for example, or whether or not he or she is crying.

The helper's telephone manner also makes a difference. We need to use the "uh-huh" response occasionally to show that we are listening, and we need to project empathy, warmth, and genuineness through our words and our tone of voice. A flat, disinterested monotone doesn't do much to show that we care. Once again, however, we must emphasize the value of "doing what comes naturally." When a helper really cares, his voice will convey this. If he couldn't care less, that will come through too.

There is one other problem with telephone counseling, and that is the tendency to engage in chatty conversation rather than in true helping.[7] To some extent the difference between conversation and counseling isn't all that great. Chatting socially with a friend can often be therapeutic, especially for people who are lonely or in need of support, but counseling is usually thought of as something more. There is a problem to be dealt with, and in dealing with it the counselor must be objective and willing to confront, teach, or guide, as necessary. This isn't always possible when a telephone call becomes no more than the social contact that we usually associate with telephone conversations.

PRACTICAL CONSIDERATIONS IN
TELEPHONE HELPING

Thus far we have tried to show that while helping over the telephone is difficult, it is also an effective way to help many people. We come now to some practical suggestions for what we can do to help people through telephone counseling, how we can avoid harmful attitudes which sometimes arise in this work, and how we can cope with problem callers.

Several years ago a published article gave some very down-to-earth guidelines for the person who counsels over the telephone. "You are limited only by your ingenuity," wrote the author. "Within this limit you can do the following:

> You can listen. It may be a rare experience for the caller; he may learn something just from having the opportunity to talk freely. . . .
>
> You can be yourself. You are selected (for telephone counseling) on the assumption that you are a good human being, and that relationships with good human beings promote growth. People in a jam need other people.
>
> You can mobilize resources, both in others and for others. The caller often possesses the answer, or the wherewithal to create it, but cannot see it. You can help him find his own answer, by helping focus the question to be answered, for example. You can also mobilize resources for him, in the sense of making referrals, making contacts with other agencies, calling a friend or minister to the rescue, sending police, setting up an appointment in the morning, and so on.
>
> You can learn your own limits and know when it is necessary to mobilize resources for yourself—when to yell for help. Always err on the generous side in using your consultants. . . .
>
> You can provide feedback. You will learn from the phone work. Share (your learning with other telephone counselors). . . .
>
> You can sympathize, question, clarify, suggest, inform, just plain be there![8]

This was written to help the volunteer who works in a telephone counseling service, but it can also apply to pastoral counselors and peer helpers. There is much about telephone counseling that is no different from any other kind of helping.

Be Alert to the Helpee's Problems

This involves asking yourself, "Why is he or she on the phone?" "What kind of help is needed?" "What can I do?" Very often, of course, we don't know what the real problem is, so we guess and then try to get facts that will prove or disprove our hypothesis. In time a clearer picture of the problem will emerge.

Be Sensitive to the Helpee's Feelings

How is he responding emotionally? Is he depressed, anxious, embarrassed, defensive, angry, suspicious, or expressing hope? Does he seem unusually placid or emotionless? What about the intensity or appropriateness of feelings? Does he show a nervous laughter or sound unusually happy while describing something sad? In all of this the helper keeps asking himself what these feelings might mean or what they might tell us about the helpee.

Be Aware of the Helpee's Thinking

What, for example, does he think is his problem? Does he have any ideas about what might be causing the problem or how it can be dealt with? What has he tried in the past? As the helpee talks, be alert to such signs of tension as rambling speech, lack of clarity, inability to concentrate, or a tendency to jump to faulty conclusions. Remember that God made us rational creatures, but that we often don't think very rationally, especially when we are under stress. *What* a person thinks and *how* he thinks can both be clues to the nature of his problem.

Be Sensitive to the Helpee's Actions

During the Second World War, Paul Tournier wrote an interesting little book on loneliness in which he suggested that a lot of loneliness is our own fault.[9] We take a "poor-little-me/no-one-cares" attitude and complain that we are victims of fate or other people's insensitivity, whereas it may be that our own attitudes and actions are driving people away and making us miserable. Not all problems are our own fault, but many are. Sin can get us into trouble, and so can inconsistent behavior and actions, which are self-defeating. Elsewhere I have described the lady who feared that she was losing her married daughter. In an attempt to prevent this, the mother reached out in a smothering and demanding way. Naturally the daughter resisted this and drew back. The mother in turn became more demanding of love and attention, so much so that she eventually drove the daughter away. By her own actions the mother brought about the result that she feared most. There are, finally, inconsistencies in behavior which can get us into trouble. Lying and trying to cover up is the clearest example, but there is also the problem of trying to believe one way and live another. "When the behavior and basic philosophy of life are at odds, the personality is usually in trouble."[10]

Be Alert to Common Counselor Errors

There are several traps into which helpers often fall if they are not careful. These failings are seen in face-to-face counseling as well as in counseling that takes place over the telephone. Consider, for example, the tendency to put an overemphasis on questions. This is perhaps the easiest trap to get into. Within five minutes from the start of an interview you can get into a question-answer routine and find yourself desperately trying to think of something else to ask in order to keep the interview going. The counselee, in turn, assumes that you will come up with a concise answer to the problem once you get all of this information. It is best to ask open-ended questions—the kind that cannot be answered in a word or two (e.g., "What's been happening lately?" or "What kinds of feelings have you been having?" instead of "Are you depressed?"). Keep the language simple, and don't be afraid to use prodding comments like "Tell me more," "What happened then?" or "That must have aroused some feelings in you."

Another common error is an overeagerness to find quick solutions. The helpee may have been struggling with his problem for a long time, so why should you think it possible to solve everything in 10 or 15 minutes? It is best to take your time and put most of the initial emphasis on listening.

It helps too if the counselor avoids clichés. These are usually used in good faith, but they can be very annoying. "I know just how you feel," "Don't worry about it," "You'll get over it," "Remember that all things work together for good," "Just pray about it" are statements which aren't very helpful to people under tension. Sometimes these clichés are accompanied by a little sermon or capsule of advice. Invariably these are well-meant, but they are seldom heeded, and more often than not they reflect insecurity on the part of a helper who doesn't know what else to do or say.

Surprising as it may seem, helpers and helpees sometimes make the error of avoiding a problem altogether. It hurts to talk about the helpee's marriage breakup, job failure, or rebellious kids, so we sometimes talk about the weather, sports, or politics instead. A couple of years ago somebody gave me a delightful little metal figurine of a counselor with his counselee on the couch. I put this on my desk but soon discovered that it was more than a conversation piece. It was a good topic for discussion which didn't so much build rapport (as I had hoped) but instead became a distraction from the more painful but necessary discussions of counselee problems.

GAMES PEOPLE HELPERS PLAY

In a somewhat tongue-in-cheek manner, one psychologist has listed some attitudes which often arise, especially in telephone counseling.[11] Borrowing from Eric Berne,[10] we might call these "games people helpers play:"

Game 1. "I've got to say something." This is the attitude which says we have to come up with a quick answer, even though such answers are often superficial and unrealistic. It is better to listen longer.

Game 2. "I better not say what I'm thinking or it might happen." This borders on superstition. It is the idea that we shouldn't raise issues of suicide, possible failure, death, or the possibility of the helpee's being sued for divorce, lest this shake the helpee and/or cause the feared event to happen. Helpees are rarely that sensitive. If a helper thinks of some pending crisis, the helpee has probably already thought of it too and might appreciate the chance to discuss the issue openly.

Game 3. "If only I knew more, I could help." This may hide our fear of failure in our helping, so we search for more information, or perhaps a Biblical proof-text that will be a key to unlocking the problem and bringing instant mental health. Counseling is hard work. Together the helper and helpee must look for answers, but it is rare to find a nugget of insight so golden that it solves the problem quickly and efficiently.

Game 4. "There must be an answer if only I can think of it." Perhaps it's not our job to think of it. We may not agree with one counselor who has suggested that "answers are created, never discovered," but there can be great frustration if we try to come up with a directive, authoritarian solution to every problem. Our job, remember, is to be the Holy Spirit's instrument in helping troubled people. This is more important than trying to be an answer man—especially a "pat" answer man.

Game 5. "There must be somebody who can help." This might be true, and for this reason referral is often wise. We must remember, however, that in many situations peer counselors are the best helpers there are. Always recognize that the helpful "somebody" might be you.

Game 6. "I am an empathetic, warm, understanding, and consistently competent counselor." This is, of course exactly what we *want* to be, but let's remember that in reality we are fallible human beings who sometimes make mistakes—even serious counseling errors. When this happens we ask the Lord to forgive us, often ask our counselees to do the same, and go on determined not to make the same mistake again.

PROBLEM CALLERS

One problem with telephone helping is that people can get to you at any hour of the day or night—including the dinner hour. This can play havoc with the counselor's own family if meals and home routines are interrupted perpetually by people who want to talk about their problems. In our house we have a rule that nobody talks on the phone during the dinner hour—especially me. To keep us from being tempted we turn the bell off at meal times. Our friends and counselees know this, and if they do call at dinner time and get no answer they simply call back later.

Even with a safeguard like this, however, some callers are insensitive to the helper's own needs and can be very difficult to handle at times.[11] Among these are the subtle, the chronic, the silent, and the obscene caller.

The Subtle Caller

The subtle caller is the one who is really asking for help but lacks the courage or willingness to come right out and say that he has a problem. According to Dr. Gene Brockopp of the Buffalo Suicide Prevention and Crisis Service[12] these subtle cries for help can take several forms. Sometimes the caller just hangs up when you answer because he wants to check out your tone of voice before speaking. Later he calls back. At other times the caller says he is calling for some friend who has a problem. Brockopp always accepts what the caller says at face value, but maintains the hypothesis that the caller himself is most likely the person with the problem. Calls for information (about suicide, mental health, or some other topic) are handled in the same way. At times people are hostile or inclined to joke about people who call for help, but this is often a defense. By reacting in a gracious or serious manner, the counselor can often get to the problem quickly. These calls are also somewhat subtle in that the caller may speak on one level but really hopes that he will get help, sympathy, and understanding for a problem that he has not yet been able to bring up. These subtle approaches are not limited to telephone counseling. They often mask face-to-face cries for help as well.

The Chronic Caller

The chronic caller is the person, often lonely or depressed, who calls several times every day. This, of course, can be very draining on the helper and very difficult to handle. We could tell such people not to call at all, or we could simply let them talk for as long as they want every time they call, but in both cases we are not likely to help them and might feel guilty frustration ourselves. Often it is helpful to set limits, perhaps stating that calls must be limited to ten minutes—and sticking to this rule. In addition, Brockopp suggests that such people be put into contact with community helping agencies, that there be plenty of support but a minimum of confrontation, that specific and concrete problems be discussed along with possible solutions (rather than letting the caller ramble on), that chronic callers be put in touch with each other or with peer helpers in the church who have more time to listen, that you suggest "writing therapy" (in which the caller writes about his problems and mails in his letters instead of talking), and that the caller be called periodically to give the reassurance that we care. One further point is that we should not feel guilty about setting some limits on the time or number of calls. This helps the caller face reality and contributes to the sanity of the counselor and his family.

The Silent Caller

The silent caller presents a different kind of problem. Here is a person who is motivated enough to call but who refuses to talk once he gets you on the phone. You as a helper then have a double problem. You are cut off from both visual and auditory clues. At such a time you could read your mail or a book—since the caller can't see you either—but it is better to encourage him a little. "Sometimes it's difficult to talk, isn't it?" is a good opener. "Is there something I can do to help?" "I would like to talk with you," or "It's hard to know what's happening when you don't talk," are all possible responses. When all else fails you might try a response like "I'd like to talk with you but I'll have to hang up in a minute or so if you can't talk." If there is still silence you might assure him of your interest and God's concern, encourage him to call again at some other time, and then say good-bye before hanging up.

The Obscene Caller

The obscene caller especially enjoys calling church leaders because he likes to shock such people and see if he can get them angry. If he can get a preacher mad it helps to convince him that religious people aren't so good—and perhaps they're as bad as he. In a strange way this contributes to his self-esteem, as does the feeling that swearing is a way to assert masculinity or one's power over other people. Getting mad at such callers is not the way to handle this situation, but neither is it appropriate to listen with "unconditional positive regard." Firmness, mixed with kindness and compassion, is probably the best approach. "I'm glad to talk with you," we might say, "but I'll have to ask you not to use that kind of language." If the caller persists, threaten to hang up, then do so. If the calls persist, the local police or telephone company should be contacted. Remember that such callers have problems, and their calls may be a hidden cry for help and understanding.

DISCIPLESHIP AND THE TELEPHONE

For obvious reasons Jesus never used the telephone in His ministry, but for us the telephone, like television and P.A. systems, is an instrument which gives us a greater opportunity to intervene in the lives of others. As with face-to-face helping, telephone helping has the same discipling goals. While it is unlikely that anyone would be discipled completely over the phone, it is technically possible. The telephone certainly can be used to give encouragement, support, advice, guidance, and confrontation. The gospel can be presented over the phone, we can pray with people over the phone, and we can encourage them in their personal and spiritual growth. Shut-ins can have a special telephone ministry, using the phone to go where they cannot go in person.

As indicated at the beginning of this chapter, most telephone helping is done by nonprofessionals. This is the peer helper's special and unique area of expertise. As such, it is an approach to helping that must not be overlooked by those whose ultimate goal in life is to fulfill the Great Commission by going into all the world to make disciples. Part of our going can well be through the telephone.

7

SUICIDE AND REFERRAL HELPING

Within the next sixty seconds somebody in North America will attempt to take his life, and, unless you are a speed reader, before you get to the end of this chapter one of these attempts will succeed—a human being will have died by his own hand. Chances are that the victim will be male, elderly, and depressed, since these people are the most successful of all in killing themselves. Suicide has been described as something which is very democratic. It is seen in the rich and the poor, the educated and the uneducated, the young and the old. And it is seen in Christians as well as in nonbelievers.

Consider Marsha, for example. Pretty and vivacious, she grew up in a Christian family and was verbal about her commitment to Christ. In high school, however, this witness began to cause trouble. Fellow students criticized Marsha for her religion and tried to pressure her into taking drugs and participating in their free-sex life-styles. Marsha felt a real inner turmoil. She talked to her Christian parents and they tried to help, but without success. Her body was found one morning in the family car, where she had died by carbon monoxide poisoning.

A THOUSAND A DAY

According to the World Health Organization approximately a thousand people around the world die every day, like Marsha, as a result of suicide.[1] These figures are probably low. In places like the United States, Canada, or Western Europe, self-destruction is not something very honorable, so death certificates rarely mention suicide if there might be some other possible explanation for the death. The official figures also hide the fact that large numbers of people try to kill themselves but fail to do so. It has been estimated that for every successful suicide there are eight or ten unsuccessful attempts. This means that roughly 10,000 people will attempt suicide someplace in the world today![2]

At some time any person who is involved in people helping will be faced with someone who is threatening suicide. Our natural reaction may be to panic or to push the helpee off to someone else. Making a referral is probably the best reaction in the long run, but sometimes this is not feasible and occasionally it is extremely unwise. Louis Dublin, who was a pioneer in suicide prevention, once remarked that the peer counselor is "probably the most important single discovery in the fifty-year history of suicide prevention. Little progress was made until he came into the picture."[3] Nonprofessional helpers have shown themselves to be very effective in helping people through the crises that lead to the consideration of suicide. The nonprofessional may therefore be the most crucially important person in helping people who are contemplating suicide. For this reason nonprofessional people helpers need all the knowledge they can get in spotting a potential suicide and deciding what to do about it.

THE NATURE OF SUICIDE

The occurrence of suicide is as old as recorded history. It is described in early Egyptian, Hebrew, and Roman writings, it was discussed by the Greek philosophers, and it has been of concern to a number of authors and theologians throughout the whole Christian era. The Bible records seven suicides,[4] of which the death of Saul and the hanging of Judas Iscariot are probably the best-known. In no place in Scripture do we see any direct evaluation of suicide, though murder is clearly condemned and, to the extent that suicide could be considered self-murder, it is a sin against God. He created life through His son (Heb. 1:1-3), He sustains life, and presumably He—not we—has the sole right to take a life in accordance with divine sovereignty.

For many people, however, there comes a time or times in life when crises are so bad and situations appear so hopeless that death is seen as the only way out. For many years the police department in Los Angeles collected the suicide notes of people who had taken their own lives, but nobody paid much attention to these until two psychologists named Edwin Shneidman and Norman Farberow began to read and analyze them. Eventually this led to the establishment of the Los Angeles Suicide Prevention Center, which, during the past two decades, has dealt with literally thousands of suicidal and potentially suicidal persons.

Based on this experience, Farberow, Shneidman, and a psychiatrist named Robert Litman have done a great deal to teach the rest of us about suicide and to show how suicide can be prevented.[5] Almost always a suicide attempt is a cry for help, a nonverbal way of saying "I'm under a lot of pressure and I don't know what else to do." The helper's job, therefore, is twofold: to judge how serious the person is about killing himself or herself, and to take some kind of action based on this evaluation.

EVALUATING SUICIDE POTENTIAL

Almost everyone who attempts suicide gives some clues of his intentions beforehand. Sometimes the clues are pretty clear—as when a person announces that he is "thinking about committing suicide." More often, however, the clues are much more subtle than this, and the helper has to be alert or he might miss them. In general the clues are of five types: verbal (what he says), behavioral (what he does), descriptive (who he is), situational (what has happened), and symptomatic (how he is coping). In evaluating the potential for suicide, the counselor must try to keep all of these things in mind.

Verbal Clues

These can be of two types. Sometimes the person comes right out and says that he is contemplating suicide. Such threats should be taken seriously. The old idea that "if he talks about it he won't do it" is an old wives' tale that has no basis in fact.

The second type of verbal clue is more subtle. Such statements as "I won't be at work next week" or "This is the last exam I'll ever study for" don't mention suicide but they strongly hint that it is a possibility. Questions like "What could I do about a friend who is thinking of killing herself?" could also be seen as a veiled clue to the questioner's own intentions.

Sometimes it is appropriate to ask a potential suicide victim if he has ever thought about how he would kill himself. In general, if he has thought about the time, place, and method, he is serious about his intentions, especially if his method is something like using a gun or jumping off a high balcony. These are methods which almost always work (assuming the gun is loaded and the balcony high enough), unlike slashing one's wrist or taking a few extra aspirin tablets. If he already owns a gun or has bought the rat poison, the threat is even greater.

Behavioral Clues

Sometimes people don't mention suicide but their emotions and actions point in that direction. Consider, first, the emotions. Most people who consider suicide are depressed and feel that life is hopeless. Once they decide to kill themselves, however, they feel more relaxed. A decision has been made, some of the pressure has been lifted, and they show a sudden and noticeable change in mood. Relatives sometimes are encouraged by this until the suicide attempt occurs.

Sometimes a person's actions reveal his intentions. Paying off old bills, updating insurance policies, giving away prized possessions like a stereo or golf clubs, and ceasing to communicate with a counselor could be behavioral indications that the person is preparing to go away permanently.

Descriptive Clues

These refer to who the person is, and such clues may or may not be helpful to the counselor. As we have seen, people of all ages and status commit suicide, but some are more prone to do so than others. In general, men commit suicide more often than women, and people over forty do so more than those who are younger. Young girls may talk about it and even make halfhearted attempts, but a man over fifty who talks about suicide is a greater threat.

To some extent the person's life-style is also important. Some people are chronic threateners. Like the little boy who cried "wolf," they threaten often, and as they get older the likelihood of their carrying through increases. In general, however, threats from these people are not as serious as those which come from people who have had stable lives and marriages. These people can often be helped over a crisis, but right now they are dead serious about suicide, and if not watched carefully they might just be dead!

Situational Clues

Before people start thinking about suicide there is usually some crisis or stress which they can't handle. Loss of a loved one, discovery of a malignancy or other serious illness, separation from children, loss of a job or status, divorce, despair over the inability to control drinking or sexual excesses, arrest, criminal involvement, destruction of property, loss of money—all of these can put a person under extreme stress. Even good things—like a promotion or graduation from college—are stressful to most people. Stress, therefore, must always be seen from the helpee's point of view, since he or she may view a situation much differently than we do.[6] When the stress is intense, the likelihood of suicide is probably also high.

Symptomatic Clues

The issue of how a person *copes* with stress is as important as the stress itself. According to Shneidman[7] there are several symptoms which indicate that the person is not coping very well. These symptoms include depression and hopelessness, disorientation or confusion, a tendency to be complaining or dissatisfied, and sometimes a defiant attitude which says, in essence, "I may be down but at least I'm in charge of ending my life when I please!" Alcoholics, drug addicts, people who are seriously ill, and those who think they have a terminal illness may all be high suicide risks, especially if they feel overwhelmed by these conditions.

THE AVAILABILITY OF HELPERS

When a person is lonely, worried, and has no one to talk to, life is a lot more difficult, and suicide much more likely, than if he has relatives and friends who are nearby and who really care. Even when such people exist, they can't help much if they have no indication that a person might be thinking about suicide. Consider, for example, dentists, physicians, and lawyers—all of whom have a higher-than-average rate of suicide even though they come into contact with people every day. What these professions have in common is a lack of other people to turn to during times of stress. People don't believe that successful professionals would contemplate suicide, and the professionals are reluctant to talk about their own inner turmoil.

In contrast, when there is someone to talk to, the likelihood of self-destruction is lowered considerably. Friends and relatives are the most obvious helpers, but there are other resources—neighbors, coworkers, church members, pastors, teachers, family physicians, private counselors, or even barbers and hairdressers. These resouce people can all help. So can the stranger who answers the phone at the suicide prevention center. So can the police who answer an emergency call. So can you!

Table 3 is a summary of some of the more common suicide clues. It can be used as a checklist to determine how serious a person is about taking his or her own life. In general, the more checkmarks on your list, the greater the danger of suicide.

◼ TABLE 3 ◼

Suicide Evaluation Checklist

Verbal
__ Open talk of suicide
__ Talk of not being present in the near future
__ Questions about suicide
__ No longer talking to counselor

Behavioral
__ Severe depression (including apathy, insomnia)
__ Sudden improvement in mental attitude
__ Guilt, shame, embarrassment
__ Feelings of hostility, revenge
__ Tension and anxiety
__ Poor judgment
__ Knowledge of available methods
__ Clearly-thought-out plans
__ Proposed method available (gun, drugs, etc.)
__ Giving away possessions
__ Buying or updating insurance
__ Paying long-standing bills
__ Putting personal affairs in order

Descriptive
__ Male
__ Over 40
__ One or more almost-successful past attempts
__ Sudden, first-time decision to kill self

Situational
__ Loss of loved person by death, divorce, separation
__ Loss of money, prestige, job (including retirement)
__ Sickness, serious illness, surgery, accident, loss of limb
__ Threat of criminal prosecution
__ Change(s) in life situation
__ Failure of counseling
__ Success, promotion, increased responsibilities

Symptomatic
__ Feelings of hopelessness
__ Dissatisfaction
__ Confused thinking
__ Tendency to complain
__ Defiant attitude
__ Drug or drinking problem
__ Inability to control impulses

Resources
__ No sources of support (friends, relatives, etc.)
__ Family, friends available but unwilling to help
__ No church or community contact
__ Living alone

PREVENTING SUICIDE

For most of us, it can be pretty scary to realize that at some time we might be talking with someone who is seriously contemplating suicide. It is not unusual, therefore, for a potential helper to back off, hoping that he has not heard correctly or that maybe the person will go someplace else with his problem. In one research study it was found that two-thirds of all suicidal persons communicated their intentions before killing themselves, but that the people who received the communications either panicked or did nothing.[8] Friends, relatives, and others who could have helped, didn't do so because they were tense, worried, or not sure what to do. Apparently they hoped that the problem would go away, but in so doing they ignored a cry for help. After the suicide these people probably felt very guilty.

The decision to commit suicide is primarily an indication that someone is in a crisis. The crisis intervention techniques discussed in chapter 5 are therefore useful in dealing with the suicidal helpee. Basically, someone is crying for help, and our task is to provide this help by listening and responding with concern and honesty. What we really need, it has been suggested, are "sharp eyes and ears, good intuition, a pinch of wisdom, an ability to act appropriately, and a deep resolve."[9] This sounds easy, but it isn't really specific enough.

Much more helpful advice is given in a little pamphlet published by the Public Affairs Committee in New York:[10]

> *Do* take seriously every suicidal threat, comment, or act. Suicide is no joke. Don't be afraid to ask the person if he is really thinking about committing suicide. The mention won't plant the idea in his head. Rather, it will relieve him to know that he is being taken seriously, that he is better understood than he suspected.
>
> *Don't* dismiss a suicidal threat and underestimate its importance. Never say "Oh, forget it. You won't kill yourself. You can't really mean it. You're not the type." That kind of remark may be a challenge to a suicidal per-

son. Such a person needs attention, not dismissal. Anyone desperate enough can be "the type."

Don't try to shock or challenge the person by saying "Oh, go ahead and do it." Such an impatient remark may be hard to hold back if a person has been repeating his threats or has been bothersome to have around. But it is a careless invitation to suicide.

Don't try to analyze the person's behavior and confront him with interpretations of his actions and feelings during the moment of crisis. That should be done later by a professional.

Don't argue with the individual about whether he should live or die. That argument can't be won. The only possible position to take is that the person *must* live.

Don't assume that time heals all wounds and everything will get better by itself. That can happen, but it can't be counted on.

Do be willing to listen. You may have heard the story before, but hear it again. Be genuinely interested, be strong, stable, and firm. Promise the person that everything possible will be done to keep him alive, because that is what he needs most.

It is not idle talk to remind the Christian helper that we have a divine source of strength and wisdom to help us and work through us as we talk to troubled people. Remember that the best way to help people is to be a friend and to use every available resource to help the troubled person cope successfully with the crisis. Often this friendship is the first step to witnessing, discipling, and showing the individual how he or she can have life in all its fullness (John 10:10) in spite of one's present difficulties.

MAKING REFERRALS

Although the peer counselor often can be extremely helpful in resolving suicidal crises, he may not be able to handle every problem that comes his way. *One of the most significant ways in which we can help people is to refer them and sometimes take them to more professional sources of help.* To do this is not an admission of failure; it is a mature recognition that none of us can help everybody. Many people can get better assistance from someone with specialized training or expertise in an area where we lack competence. If we are really interested in helping people we will not be resistant to the idea of making referrals.

Let's return for a minute to the topic of suicide. If we learn that someone has taken an overdose of pills we obviously don't sit with him showing empathy and warmth. We get him to a hospital, contact his doctor if possible, and then try to get in touch with a relative. The immediate aim is to get medical attention as soon as possible. If we can't get to the person ourselves we may have to call an ambulance, the police, or a local suicide prevention center and request their intervention.

This need to refer also occurs, of course, in less traumatic settings. Our job is to provide short-term support and encouragement while we get the helpee to someone who can do a better job as a helper. To do this we should try to keep the answers to three basic questions in mind: Where do I refer? When do I refer? How do I refer?

Where to Refer

Ministers and professional counselors often have a file of people and places to whom our helpees can be referred. The peer helper usually lacks this information, although he can often get suggestions if he calls an experienced local counselor. In remote geographical areas the range of choices may be limited, but in larger metropolitan centers the possibilities are almost endless.

Private practitioners often represent the first line of action. Psychiatrists, psychologists, and certified psychiatric social workers, for example, are counselors who can be found listed in the yellow pages of the telephone book. Do not limit your referrals to these professionals, however. Sometimes the counselee needs a good general practitioner, dentist, lawyer or banker to help with a problem. And very often the counselee can get the greatest help from a pastor.

Apart from the pastor, private practitioners often charge high fees, and this might have a bearing on where you refer. Remember too that professionals often unite together in clinics or groups which can provide help.

Community agencies are another source of help. Some of these, like mental health clinics, psychiatric hospitals, or outpatient psychiatric departments in a general hospital, deal primarily with personal problem situations. Marriage clinics, of course, deal with troubled marriages, and drug centers also have a specialized emphasis. There are also agencies which are helpful to people but do not deal with so-called mental illness. Vocational guidance centers, employment agencies, legal aid societies, welfare agencies, and many of the United Fund agencies provide community help, often at minimal cost. Groups like the society for the blind or the local retarded children's society should not be overlooked, and neither should government agencies, like the division of vocational rehabilitation or the department of welfare. The state welfare department can often provide guidance in finding other referral sources if in itself it cannot help.

Lay organizations can also assist with referrals. Alcoholics Anonymous, for example, is probably the best place to refer the problem drinker who wants help. A. A. also has groups for the spouses and children of alcoholics. Groups like TOPS (Take Off Pounds Sensibly), or Recovery, Inc. (to help former mental patients) are so influential that one psychologist has written a whole book about their effectiveness.[11] Table 4 on next page lists some of the most frequently used referral services.

In making referrals the Christian is faced with a very basic concern: how does the counselor or group to whom I refer view religion? We are making an unjustified assumption if we conclude that all non-Christian counselors are opposed to religion and determined to undermine the faith of their counselees, although it is true that this sometimes does happen. It is also true that many Christian psychologists or other professionals may use a therapeutic

━━━━━━━━━━ **TABLE 4** ━━━━━━━━━━

Where to Refer

There can be a variety of referral sources in any given community. Most of these are listed in the telephone directory. The State Welfare agency can often provide referral information in addition to the following suggestions:

Problem	Consider Referral to:
alcoholism	Alcoholics Anonymous, general hospital, physician, psychiatrist, Salvation Army
child abuse, need	State Department of Children and Family Services, Child Welfare Agency
depression, bizarre behavior, anxiety, confusion, etc.	psychologist, psychiatrist, mental health clinic
drug problem	general hospital, counseling clinic, psychiatrist
financial	state or local welfare agency, United Fund office, churches, bank, loan company
handicap	Society for the Blind, Retarded Children's Society, United Fund office, local service club
legal problems	lawyer, legal aid society
marriage problem	marriage counselor, psychologist, social worker, counseling clinic, pastor
missing person	police department
physical problem	physician
poisoning	general hospital
pregnancy	physician, pastor
spiritual problem	pastor
suicide threat	suicide prevention center, psychologist, psychiatrist, mental health clinic, pastor
vocational	private employment agency, state department of vocational rehabilitation, school guidance counselor, psychologist

approach which differs very little from the approach of non-Christian counselors. Our desire is to see individuals become disciples and disciplers. It is difficult, therefore, to see how progress can be made toward this goal if the counselor has a purely secular set of goals, or if he has never heard about discipleship.

Let us not forget, however, that God is sovereign and powerful. He does not require people—including you and me—to have perfect theology before we are used. If we search the Scriptures we find that God sometimes even uses nonbelievers to accomplish His divine purposes. A non-Christian counselor, like a nonbelieving physician or lawyer, may at times use his or her professional skill to guide a counselee through a crisis or to help restructure a personality, both of which may get the person to a point where he or she is more ready to accept Christ and move toward becoming a disciple. Sometimes physical or psychological problems must be dealt with before we can come to the spiritual, and we have pointed out previously that all these aspects of the personality are important.

Nevertheless, to refer someone to a non-Christian or uncommitted counselor can indeed be harmful at times, and for this reason every attempt should be made to find someone who follows Biblically-based principles of therapy. To be realistic, we must recognize that such persons are rare, and that at times we will have to settle for a professional who has a nonjudgmental attitude toward religion. God sometimes uses such people to bring about a healing which ultimately allows the helpee to grow properly as a disciple.

When to Refer

There was a time, several years ago, when professional counselors routinely suggested that all counseling problems should be referred. O. Hobart Mowrer, a past president of the American Psychological Association, challenged this view in a controversial little book which suggested that

Christians, even Christian laymen, could bring a healing spiritual dimension to counseling which no secular therapist could match.[12] When research began to appear showing the effectiveness of peer counselors and the insufficient numbers of professional counselors, more and more people began to conclude that referral might not always be the best thing. Sometimes it is better for the dedicated helper to stick with a helpee, perhaps with occasional advice from a more experienced counselor.

Nevertheless, referral is necessary when the present helper lacks the time, the emotional stamina or stability, and the skill or experience to continue the counseling. As a general rule, we should refer whenever we don't seem to be helping someone deal with the problem of life or to grow as a whole person. More specifically, it is important to seek outside help for counselees who:
  —are in legal difficulties
  —have severe financial needs
  —require medical attention
  —are severely depressed or suicidal
  —will require more time than we can give
  —want to shift to another counselor
  —show extremely aggressive behavior
  —make excessive use of drugs or alcohol
  —arouse strong feelings of dislike, sexual stimulation, or
    threat in the counselor
  —appear to be severely disturbed.

It is sometimes very easy to spot a severely disturbed person, but in other situations the disturbance is less obvious. One writer has given the following concise list of symptoms which may indicate the presence of a severe disturbance:

(a) The person believes that others are attempting to harm him, assault him sexually, or influence him in strange ways. (b) He has delusions of grandeur about himself. (c) He shows abrupt changes in his typical pattern of behavior. (d) He hears voices, sees visions, or smells odors which do not exist. (e) He has rigid, bizarre ideas and fears which cannot be influenced by logic. (f) He engages in a repetitious pattern of compulsive actions or obsessive thoughts. (g) He is disoriented (unaware of time, place, or personal identity). (h) He is depressed to the point of near-stupor or is strangely elated and/or aggressive. (i) He withdraws into his inner world, losing interest in normal activities.[13]

When symptoms such as these appear, referral would be a wise alternative.

How to Refer

Referral is not something that helpees always accept enthusiastically, especially if they originally came to you for help and a good relationship has been built up. It is important, therefore, that the helpee should not feel rejected or "passed off" to somebody else. To make the referral process as smooth as possible, several guidelines might be kept in mind.

First, involve the helpee in the decision to refer. Remember that the helper and helpee are coworkers, trying to solve some problems. You should decide jointly how the problems can be solved most effectively, and this may involve using another helper. If the present helper brings up this idea first, he should do so gently, giving the helpee plenty of time to respond.

Second, the helper can pave the way by finding out what community resources are available, what they cost, and whether or not they have a waiting list. It is probably better if the helpee makes his own appointment with the new counselor, though this is not a hard and fast rule.

Third, discuss the relationship that you will have following the referral. In professional circles, the former counselor usually takes a "hands off" attitude when the new counselor takes over. With pastoral or peer counseling, however, this isn't always necessary. There can still be contact, especially on a friendly, supportive, or pastoral basis, though the new counselor or group accepts the major counseling responsibility.

Bible Referrals

This whole idea of making referrals is as old as the Bible. Perhaps the most interesting example occurred when the children of Israel were camped at the foot of Mount Horeb in the middle of their wilderness travels (Exod. 18). Moses discovered that he was spending all of his time judging the people, hearing complaints and settling disputes. Undoubtedly this was mostly legal counseling, but perhaps some personal problems were brought to Moses too.

Jethro, Moses' father-in-law, was visiting at the time and watched all of this with increasing concern because Moses was apparently wearing himself out as a people helper (Exod. 18:18). Finally Jethro intervened with some advice of his own. Choose some able, God-fearing helpers, Jethro suggested, who are truthful, honest, available at all times, and willing to help with the counseling. When the problems get too difficult, these helpers will make referrals to a more experienced counselor (Exod. 18:26).

This is a good model for today. Skilled, Spirit-filled men and women of God have the privilege of helping each other. But with this privilege goes the responsibility of referring difficult cases to others with greater expertise. To refer is sometimes the best way to help.

8

PREVENTIVE HELPING

There are a lot of ways in which we can help people. Counseling, of course, is one of these ways. Sensitive, willing helpers can do a great deal to assist others as they cope with problems, deal with crises, and learn how to get along better in the future.

Sometimes, however, people helping has nothing to do with crises or emotional problems. Helping a friend move, watching the neighbor's kids for an afternoon, or assisting a fellow student with a term paper are all helpful acts which make life a little easier for someone else.

Another kind of helping is what we want to discuss in this chapter. It is a kind of helping which isn't discussed very often in counseling books, though it is every bit as important as the more traditional counseling. It is known by various names—preventive psychiatry, for example, or community psychology—but its purpose is to prevent problems and crises from developing in the first place.

The prevention of problems may or may not involve psychiatry and psychology. It usually involves whole communities, although this is not always necessary. It sometimes involves counseling, but not always. Because we lack a better term, let us use "preventive helping" to describe this whole enterprise of helping people to steer clear of potential problems.

THE AIMS OF PREVENTIVE HELPING

Preventive helping is usually seen as having three aims.[1] First, preventive helping attempts to *prevent problems* from happening in the first place. This is sometimes called primary prevention, and it involves both anticipating problem situations before they occur and changing or avoiding conditions which might give rise to problems. Premarital counseling is an excellent example of this kind of prevention. While the couple is still anticipating marriage, both parties are alerted to potential problems between husbands and wives and are given instructions on how to prevent such problems from occurring.

Second, preventive helping attempts to *arrest or stop existing problems* before they get worse. This is called secondary prevention, and it involves cutting the duration and the severity of a developing problem. When a church holds marriage-enrichment seminars for married couples, it is often engaging in secondary prevention. Problems which might have been developing are identified and dealt with before they get worse.

It is very difficult for an outsider to stop developing problems in the life of someone else. In their early stages, developing problems are often hidden—sometimes even from the person who has them—and for an outsider to intervene is often seen as meddling. People who do admit that they have developing problems often do not want help, since they feel that they can handle the situation themselves. Sometimes they don't even want to change. Drinking or promiscuous sexual behavior might be pleasant at first, and people who engage in these activities often prefer to be left alone.

A third kind of preventive helping, known sometimes as tertiary prevention, tries to reduce or *eliminate the influences of previous problems*. Suppose, for example, that a former alcoholic, mental patient, or prisoner returns to his or her hometown and tries to get a job. Very often such a person encounters suspicion from others, criticism, prejudice, lack of acceptance, and a great deal of mistrust. This can be devastating to the person who is trying to move back into the community and return to a normal life. In such situations, people helpers can work with both the individual and the community to make the transition smoother and to prevent a rejection which might lead the returning person to become so discouraged that he returns to his former ways.

PREVENTION IN THE CHURCH AND COMMUNITY

Until recently, evangelicals have said almost nothing about the problem of prevention, even though the Bible is filled with practical advice on how both the church and individual believers can avoid problems and live more stable lives. It is possible, of course, that many religious leaders see prevention as such an integral part of the church's program that it need not be considered in detail. But as Clinebell and others have shown, through worship services, Sunday school classes, "fellowship" gatherings, and business meetings the church could be doing a much better job in preventing problems. Certainly churches are not always bastions of mental stability. They are often characterized by conflict, gossip, criticism, and other sources of stress which create division in the body and tension within the members. In contrast, the church could and should be a therapeutic community. As a local body of believers, the church should contribute to the mental health and stability of every member and should be concerned about ways in which individual problems can be prevented.

Unlike some other forms of helping, prevention most often occurs outside the formal interview. When a pastor talks to his congregation about resisting the Devil, when the youth director talks to the high school group about finding God's will in one's vocation, or when the pastor's wife talks to a group about being fulfilled as a woman, preventive helping is taking place. The same occurs when a Campus Crusade leader chats with a college student about the Spirit-filled life or when a Navigator or Inter-Varsity staff worker shows a group of students how to have a regular quiet time. The high school worker who chats over a Coke with some freshman about his mounting sexual urges is likewise engaging in preventive helping, even though neither person may stop to realize that their conversation is a form of counseling which may be preventing future problems.

It should not be assumed that preventive helping focuses exclusively on individuals. On the contrary, prevention can involve both individuals or whole communities. We can, for example, help specific individuals to avoid problems, to stop problems which are developing, or to readjust following the resolution of a previous problem, but we can also work with whole groups or neighborhoods. Through government or other intervention we can work toward avoiding or reducing economic depression, acts of crime, moral degeneration in the news media, or other harmful social conditions. As a result whole societies can avoid a potential stress and can become more stable and less tense.

Most of the professional interest in the problem of prevention has had this focus on the whole society. There is now a field of study known as community psychology and another termed community psychiatry. People who work in these areas seek an active involvement in the society, including politics, service clubs, educational institutions, and the news media. By changing the society to make it less stressful, it is assumed that personal problems will be prevented, that existing difficulties will be reduced or even eliminated, and that the general level of mental health in a community will be improved.

It is interesting that the community psychology movement places great emphasis on schools, hospitals, and social service agencies but says very little about the role of the local church in the prevention of psychological disorders. In a recent book which is intended as "an introduction to the field of community psychology,"[2] the church or religion isn't even mentioned in the index and is generally ignored in the text. This could be due to the narrow-mindedness of the community-minded psychologists, but it may be equally due to the church's failure to be more involved in the prevention of psychological problems.

Undoubtedly the most prominent leader in the field of preventive pastoral psychology is Howard Clinebell, who has written one book in this area and edited another.[3] Clinebell describes the community mental health movement as "an exciting social revolution" which has "profound human significance" and "is one of the most important social revolutions in the history of our country, perhaps of the world."[4] This enthusiasm stems from the belief that by changing the community we can not only help people who are suffering from overt or hidden psychological problems, but we can also do a great deal to prevent psychological difficulties from arising in people who are well-adjusted today. In creative ways, Clinebell has shown how the church can play a significant role in changing the society and in providing an environment where mental health will be stimulated.

This concept of prevention through social intervention has been very popular among the more liberal churches. In one sense it is a new form of the old social gospel. Change the society, it argues, and we change the mental health of individuals. Evangelicals would for the most part agree that it is desirable to change the society and eliminate poverty, racial injustice, and other stress-producing conditions, but they would insist that the spiritual needs of individuals must also be met if there is to be greater mental stability and the prevention of problems.

PREVENTIVE HELPING AND DISCIPLESHIP

Nowhere is the issue of preventive counseling more clearly illustrated than in the area of discipleship. The disciple is being trained to cope with future stresses, deal with internal tensions, grow spiritually, and eventually move toward the goal of spiritual and psychological maturity.

Mental health is sometimes defined as physical, intellectual, social, and spiritual maturity. Jesus is described in the Bible as a Person who grew in stature (physically), in wisdom (intellectually), in favor with God (spiritually), and in favor with men (socially). He was the epitome of good mental health, and He trained His disciples to meet their future problems in a healthy and creative manner.

Matthew 10 gives a superb example of the preventive counseling techniques that Jesus used. At this point He was preparing to send out the twelve disciples on a short training mission, and before they left He prepared them for what they would encounter. By alerting them to potential problems, He enabled them to avoid difficulties that might otherwise have arisen. This dealing with problems before they arise is real prevention, and from Jesus' example we have a clear model on how we too can help others to prevent problems. Jesus prevented future problems for the disciples by giving encouragement, by warning them about what was coming, by telling them what to do if opposition came, by giving them some experience in facing problems, by showing them how He handled stress, by discussing their potential problems with them, and by emphasizing that relaxation is a good way to build up resistance against future stress. Let's consider each of these in turn.

Encouragement

The disciples may have been nervous and uncertain about their ability to carry on the work that Jesus had begun and expected them to continue. So He reassured them (Matt. 10:19, 26, 29-31), told them that their ministry was important (Matt. 10:40), and gave them the authority and power to face their future with confidence (Matt. 10:1; Luke 9:1). Perhaps this seems like a little thing, but the encouragement and prayerful support of another human being can be a sustaining influence which helps people as they face the future, try new ventures, change behavior, or otherwise deal with problems before they get worse.

Warning

The preparation that Jesus gave involved much more than encouragement. It warned of dangers to come. To serve me, Jesus said, will be dangerous (Matt. 10:16, 17). It might lead to disruption of families or to rejection by the people whom we love (Matt. 10:21, 22, 34-36). Those words were not just scare tactics; they were a clear statement of the dangers that Jesus' disciples could expect to face in the future.

Paul used a similar approach in Romans 16:19 when he wrote, "I want you to be wise in what is good, and innocent in what is evil" (v. 19). This gives no support to the idea that our warnings need to go into a lot of detail about the dangers that are ahead. Such detail can be harmful. We are to be "innocent in what is evil," yet alert enough to know what to avoid.

When we are warned that there are dangers ahead, we can make efforts to steer clear of problems that might arise. The church has recognized this for centuries and has warned people about the dangers of involvement in compromising sex situations, dabbling in occult practices, maintaining self-centered attitudes in marriage, or uncritically accepting the teaching at secular universities. Regretfully, these warnings aren't always received with gratitude or enthusiasm—especially when the warning comes to young people from older people. However, even if the warning goes unheeded for the moment, it is sometimes remembered at a later time, and even this can be helpful. "I was warned about this," we might think, "so I'm not surprised." To be forewarned is often a help in avoiding or stopping problems before they get worse.

Instruction

To warn a person that there is danger ahead may prevent a tradegy, but the help is even more beneficial if we can help the person to find some alternatives which are less dangerous. Jesus warned the disciples but then He did not leave them to fend for themselves. He told them specifically

   —what to do when difficult situations arise (Matt. 10:6-8, 11-14, 23)

   —what not to do in times of stress (Matt. 10:5b, 9, 10)

   —what to say when problems come (Matt. 10:27)

   —how to handle feelings (Matt. 10:28).

This is a beautiful guideline for a discipling program, but it also illustrates that part of the preventive helper's job is to educate people. To prevent problems, the helper can give instruction on such topics as how they can mature spiritually, improve their marriages, prepare for death, handle their impulses, meet frustrations, or cope with stress.

One problem with this educational type of helping is that we easily can be too superficial with our advice, too simplistic, or not really practical. All of these lead many people to think that there can be cookbook recipes for avoiding problems. This, of course, is not possible.

Another problem with instructive helping is that it can create problems which might not be there otherwise. Consider, for example, the oft-quoted statement that "97 percent of all college men masturbate and the other 3 percent are liars." What does this do to the freshman who has never thought about masturbating? Does it lead him into a problem which he might otherwise have avoided? This question has been raised by critics of sex education programs, who fear that a little knowledge can arouse curiosity which could create problems that might otherwise be avoided.

While this kind of risk surely exists, there is greater risk in keeping silent. Young people are not nearly so naive as their parents sometimes assume. Even to arouse doubt or curiosity might not be bad. It is better to have this take place while a mature helper is around than at some later time when the learner is alone and perhaps defenseless.

One other problem with giving instruction is something that concerns me whenever I teach a course, give a lecture, or write a book: will any of this make a practical difference in people's lives? Most of us have had the experience of reading a book or hearing a sermon, concluding that "this is very helpful," and then promptly forgetting what we learned. There is a lot of research to show that the passive recipient of learning won't change nearly as much as the person who absorbs the new learning and acts on it immediately and in a practical way. Jesus followed this active-learning principle in preparing His disciples for the future.

Experience

Imagine what a football team would be like if its training consisted solely of encouragement, warning of danger, and lectures on how to defeat the opposition! This is exactly how many churches, parents, and educational institutions attempt to prepare people to face the problems of life: with talk but with no practical training. Little wonder there is so much defeat!

In contrast to this, Jesus gave His disciples something to do. He sent them out for practical experience (Luke 9:2; 10:1) and guided them as they went.

It is not easy to provide experience for people who are learning, and at times it isn't even ethical. Sometimes we can provide artificial learning situations, such as we do in theological schools, where students preach to each other, witness to each other, or counsel with each other before going out into the nearby community. But it is difficult, if not impossible, for example, to give experience in avoiding adultery or in staying clear of the occult.

As we encourage a person to act, in those situations where training is possible, we might begin by getting their suggestions about what to do and what not to do. Together, the helper and helpee might evaluate these suggestions and try to think of some others. Then we can discuss the "how to do it" and the dangers or potential for failure that are involved. As the person tries to take action we can stick with him and perhaps even go with him as he moves out to get experience. This, of course, is what often happens as people are trained to witness. After the instruction, and perhaps some practice, they go out like the followers of Jesus, two by two.

Jesus was more than a lecturer. In preparing His disciples to anticipate and cope with the stresses of their future ministry, He did not hide His involvement. He rejoiced in their successes, helped them learn from their failures, prayed for them, and took obvious delight in their ministries (Luke 10:18-23).

Demonstration

Jesus was a model to His disciples (Matt. 11:1). He showed them how to disciple others, how to cope with problems that existed, and how to avoid potentially dangerous situations. His example must have been very helpful to them as they faced problems alone in the future.

We all know of people whose lives have inspired others. This is another way to be a people helper: showing how to live so that others can have a model to follow in the future when they face stress.

Evaluation

Learning is always more effective when there is some kind of evaluation or feedback. Athletes learned this a long time ago, studies of learning support it, and Jesus demonstrated it. When the followers of Jesus returned after their training session, they gave a report and doubtless spent time evaluating their efforts (Luke 9:10; 10:17).

Relaxation

Jesus was a very busy man, but in the midst of all the demands on His time, He took time to relax. In Luke 9:10

we read that after the disciples returned from their ministry and gave a report, Jesus "taking them with Him . . . withdrew privately." Might this have been part of the training program? Might this have been a lesson in preventive helping—showing that we should take time to rest so we are better prepared to face future problems as they arise?

We live in a time when almost everyone is busy and the whole society moves quickly. Our bodies can take only so much of this change, and if we fail to relax we become much more subject to physical illness, tension, and difficulties in getting along with people. Even our spiritual lives suffer when we fail to rest periodically—to be still while we get to know God better.

We cannot be effective people helpers when we ourselves are rushed and somewhat overwhelmed by the pressures of life. One of the best ways we can help others to avoid problems is by encouraging them to take the time to relax periodically—with a good book, a game or hobby of some sort, a respected friend, or perhaps alone by themselves. This is an essential part of preventive helping. If we are rested we face the problems of the future with greater confidence and efficiency. And the place to start is with the helper—who shows others how it is done.

GUIDELINES FOR PREVENTION

What can we conclude about the prevention of psychological and spiritual problems?

1. The best way to handle personal problems is to stop them before they begin. When this fails we should intervene early in a problem to stop it from getting worse.

2. The church is in a unique position to anticipate problems before they develop, to alert people to problems which might be ahead, to spot problems which might be developing, and to intervene to prevent existing problems from getting worse.

3. Christians should recognize that prevention of

individual problems will require a number of attitudes on the part of the helper:

foresight—to see a potential or developing problem before it arises or gets worse.

knowledge—of how a stressful situation or environment can be changed, of where someone might be referred, and of what might be done about a developing problem situation.

courage—to get involved in trying to resolve newly developing problems—problems which because of more pressing issues we often ignore or overlook.

tact—in bringing up sensitive issues which people might not want to discuss, and in not taking a holier-than-thou or know-it-all attitude. People don't always like to be bothered about personal problems which are developing but are not yet serious.

compassion—which expresses so much concern and love for others that we are even willing to risk being rejected if this will help prevent a problem.

planning—so that dating, premarital, premiddle-age or pre-retirement issues can be raised in a nonthreatening but forceful way, and so that marriage-enrichment seminars, spiritual-growth meetings, or sharing groups can be introduced in a way that will maximize the benefits to the participants and minimize the threat for the resistant people—the ones who are the most likely to need the benefits.

4. Every aspect of the church's ministry—preaching, teaching, evangelism, social gatherings, music, business meetings, etc.—should be planned in view of the present and future spiritual and psychological welfare of the participants.

5. Education is an important part of prevention. Christian people helpers must give serious consideration to ways in which we can educate people about such issues as how to have a better marriage; how to handle family conflicts; how to cope with stress; how to avoid backbiting, gossip, and other behaviors which create problems; how to

be forgiving when people fall into sin; or how to get along with people. Jesus and the New Testament writers dealt with practical problems such as these, but contemporary Christians often ignore them. To do so is to let problems grow which otherwise might be prevented or stopped in the beginning.

The Great Commission is a beautiful example of preventive psychology. Jesus knew that living in this world was difficult, so He provided some guidelines which would help us achieve maximum stability and benefit in our lives.

"Remember," He said in essence, "that I have all power and authority." This gives us *reassurance*.

"Go and make disciples"—this gives us a real *purpose* for living.

"Baptize and teach"—this gives us the *pattern* to follow.

"Remember the three Persons of the Trinity"—this creates *stability* and a reminder of the great God we serve.

"I am with you always, even to the end of the age"—this gives a sure *hope* for the present and future.

Paul was a man who had everything the world could give—status, education, riches, self-confidence. But he became a disciple of Jesus Christ and a discipler of others. As such he was able to endure all kinds of problems and he helped others to do the same. In his Second Letter to Timothy, Paul gave some directions to his young disciple about preventing problems in himself and others. These directions are still relevant today:

Be diligent to present yourself approved to God as a workman who does not need to be ashamed, handling accurately the Word of truth. But avoid worldly and empty chatter, for it will lead to further ungodliness. . . .

Flee from youthful lusts, and pursue after righteousness, faith, love, and peace, with those who call on the Lord from a pure heart.

But refuse foolish and ignorant speculations, knowing that they produce quarrels.

And the Lord's bondservant must not be quarrelsome,

but be kind to all, able to teach, patient when wronged, with gentleness correcting those who are in opposition; if perhaps God may grant them repentance leading to the knowledge of the truth, and they may come to their senses and escape from the snare of the devil, having been held captive by him to do his will.

— 2 Timothy 2:15, 16, 22-26

9
THE BODY AS A HELPING COMMUNITY

During His ministry on earth, Jesus was very much concerned about healing. In talking to some of His critics, He made the oft-quoted comment that He had come not to minister to those who were well, but to those who needed to be healed (Mark 2:17). One fifth of all the verses in the first five books of the New Testament deal with healing,[1] and in the Gospels more attention is given to the healing ministry of Jesus than to any other subject except the events surrounding the crucifixion and resurrection.[2]

In considering these Biblical healings it is interesting to note that they almost always took place in the presence of other people. When individuals were healed, other people were usually there to watch. Sometimes the sick person was brought by others, and at times a concerned relative or friend came to Jesus to ask healing for a loved one.

In the preceding pages we have talked about psychological-spiritual healing and about helping as an interaction between two people—the helper and the person being helped. We know, of course, that counselors sometimes work in pairs, and that counselees are often helped as part of a larger group. But even in these small group situations, helping occurs pretty much independently of anyone outside the group. Might it be, however, that helping can be more effective when it takes place within the setting of a group or community of concerned people?

THE EFFECTIVENESS OF GROUP HELPING

Psychologists discovered the effectiveness of group

helping many years ago. Mental patients who had been chained in unsanitary asylums were found to improve dramatically when they were treated with compassion and kindness. As part of something called "moral treatment," the hospital administrators and staff lived with the patients, ate with them, and showed that the hospital could be a therapeutic community instead of a prison-like dungeon.[3] This idea was extended further after World War Two, when a British psychiatrist named Maxwell Jones[4] published an account of a therapeutic community in which all of the patient's daily activities were directed toward his or her recovery. "Milieu therapy" was a term which applied to this kind of treatment. One-to-one counseling was part of the treatment, but equally important was the daily support, help, and encouragement given by the staff and the patients to each other.

Milieu Therapy

Milieu therapy made a number of interesting assumptions about the helping relationship.[5] It assumed first that activities such as living together, working, or participating in recreational activities could be very therapeutic in themselves. Second, it was assumed that patients should be given responsibility—for keeping the hospital clean, planning ward activities, deciding hospital policies, and evaluating each other's progress. A third assumption was that all of the staff were to be of equal importance. The opinion and influence of a ward aide was given as much weight as that of the psychiatrist. Fourth, it was discovered that patients got better faster when the ward had an atmosphere of openness, honesty, warmth, acceptance, and interpersonal caring. Finally, there was open, two-way communication between and among the patients and staff. Disagreements were brought out into the open, where they could be dealt with in a straightforward way.

The Therapeutic Community

This idea of a therapeutic community to back up and sometimes replace individual counseling has been expanded more recently in a book titled *The Healing Community*,[6] in which the author shows how a group can help the sufferer to express hurts, to change behavior, to follow the example of more experienced or mature members of the community, and to become part of a cohesive and healing group.

What many of these psychological writers have missed, however, is that Jesus and the New Testament writers gave a model of the ideal healing community many centuries ago. The assumptions of moral and milieu therapy were first stated in the Bible, but for some reason Christians have failed to follow the Scriptural model. As a result the church has neglected its role as a therapeutic or helping community. It has, instead, tended to become a listless organization where counseling is left to the pastor or a few laymen and where people in need of help are often ignored or rejected, especially if they are not active church members or if they show unusual mannerisms.

THE NATURE OF THE BODY OF CHRIST

When Jesus was on earth He ministered through His own physical body. Wherever He went, He healed, counseled, showed compassion, taught, and lived a life which was a model for others to follow. When Jesus went back to heaven following His resurrection, His physical body disappeared from earth, but He left another body to carry on His work. This new body of Christ, which still exists today, is the church.[7]

A Faulty View of the Church

Modern men and women have developed a faulty view of the church. Many see it as an irrelevant organization of pious or hypocritical people who believe in God but are mainly concerned about adding members, developing programs, politicking in the society, and erecting bigger and bigger buildings which stand vacant for most of the week. This description is perhaps overdrawn, but it does present an image of the church which is held today even by some of its most faithful attendees.

A Biblical View of the Church

Clearly this is far from the model of the church described in the Bible. The church is supposed to be a body of believers who have committed their lives to Jesus Christ and have been equipped with spiritual gifts which each person discovers and develops (Eph. 4; 1 Pet. 4:10). These gifts, which are listed in Romans 12, 1 Corinthians 12, and Ephesians 4, include such things as prophesying, teaching, evangelizing, helping, exhorting (which, as we have seen, is very similar to counseling), tongues, healing, faith, wisdom, knowledge, discernment, showing mercy, administration, and giving. These gifts come directly from the Holy Spirit, who gives according to His will (1 Cor. 12:11).

According to Ephesians 4:12, 13 the gifts of the Spirit have two purposes. First they are to prepare individual believers for service as a part of the body of Christ. Jesus came to evangelize, to enlighten, to release those who were in bondage, and to proclaim the truth (Luke 4:18). The modern body of Christ has a similar function, and, just as the Holy Spirit empowered Jesus (Luke 4:18), so the Spirit also empowers us and gives us gifts which enable us to minister to one another.

The second purpose of spiritual gifts is to build up the body of Christ so we can be unified, knowledgeable, and mature men and women. Such people are not tossed about by the most recent fad or philosophy of life. They are stable, loving people whose lives are centered in Christ (Eph. 4:12-16).

The Authentic People Helper

Now what does all this have to do with being an authentic people helper? Simply this: one of the major purposes of the body of Christ is to help people. "God has so composed the body . . . that there should be no division in the body, but that the members should have the same care for one another. And if one member suffers, all the members suffer with it; if one member is honored, all the members rejoice with it. Now you [that is, believers] are Christ's body, and individually members of it" (1 Cor. 12:24-27). According to God's plan, the church is to be a united body of believers who are given power by the Holy Spirit, are growing to maturity, and are ministering to (i.e., helping) people both inside and outside the body.

HELPING AND THE BODY OF CHRIST

The body of Christ exists for a number of purposes, all of which can have a great helping influence on individuals. When it is fully functioning the body provides:

Fellowship

Many people in need of help are basically lonely, longing for some kind of in-depth relationship with another human being. This kind of fellowship is exactly what the body of Christ provides. Believers have fellowship with the God of the universe (according to the Bible this automatically leads to joy), and with one another (1 John 1:3, 4, 7). This kind of fellowship, which characterized the early church, arose because people had a common commitment to Christ (1 Cor. 1:9). Such a commitment and closeness ought to exist today.

> Our Christian fellowship should be directed toward building us up as Christians. . . . In the fellowship that Christians have with one another, God wants to create a

loving community that will be a witness to the non-Christian world. . . . We can give the world conclusive proof of God's operation in our lives if our fellowship together is marked by that loving, sharing quality which is markedly absent in the world at large.[8]

Regretfully, this quality is often absent in the church at large, but it shouldn't be. The body of Christ has tremendous potential for providing the kind of fellowship, acceptance, feeling of belonging, and security that brings great therapeutic value both to believers and to other needy people who come into contact with believers.

Service

Jesus was once asked how a person could attain greatness, and His reply was somewhat surprising. The way to be great, He said, is to become a servant (Matt. 20:26; Mark 9:35). This idea comes up repeatedly in the New Testament. Christians are to be submissive to one another and to serve one another.

This is an *other-centered* rather than a *self-centered* way of living. It is a life-style which, if practiced consistently, would lead to a series of mutual helping relationships. It would cause all Christians to be concerned about bearing one another's burdens (Gal. 6:2), weeping and rejoicing together (Rom. 12:15), confessing sins to each other, and praying for one another (James 5:16).

Ray Stedman has commented on this in his book *Body Life*.

> What is terribly missing is the experience of "body life," that warm fellowship of Christian with Christian which the New Testament calls *koinonia*, and which was an essential part of early Christianity. The New Testament lays heavy emphasis upon the need for Christians to know each other closely and intimately enough to be able to bear one another's burdens, confess faults one to another, rebuke, exhort, and admonish one another, minister to one another with the Word through song and prayer and thus come to . . . know the love of Christ which surpasses knowledge (Eph. 3:18, 19).[9]

Love

This, as we have seen, is the basic mark of a Christian (John 13:35), and we are instructed repeatedly to be loving people (e.g., Matt. 22:39; 1 Thes. 4:9, 10). The Biblical description of love as recorded in 1 Corinthians 13 presents us with a high standard. Love, we read, is "very patient and kind, never jealous or envious, never boastful or proud, never haughty or selfish or rude. Love does not demand its own way. It is not irritable or touchy. It does not hold grudges and will hardly even notice when others do it wrong. It is never glad about injustice, but rejoices whenever truth wins out. If you love someone," the Bible continues, "you will be loyal to him no matter what the cost. You will always believe in him, always expect the best of him, and always stand your ground in defending him (1 Cor. 13:4-7, *The Living Bible*).

Several years ago Harvard psychologist Gordon Allport called love "incomparably the greatest psychotherapeutic agent."[10] He went on to suggest that the church knows more about this than any secular counselor, but he decried the "age-long failure of religion to turn doctrine into practice."[11]

The body of Christ should be characterized by love—love for ourselves, our neighbors, our families, and even our enemies. Jesus loved us and died for us even while we were still sinners (Rom. 5:8). If this divine love were to flow through Christians and reach out to others—like it should—the results would be incredibly therapeutic.

But to love like this is risky. It takes time and effort and it might inconvenience us. So instead we talk about love but do very little about it.

Growth

The body of Christ is to be a growing, maturing group of people. They are not to be like children, but instead they are to grow together as a working unit, becoming more and more like Christ, who is Head of the body (Eph. 4:13-16).

Consider what this kind of community could do for the person who needs help. It could

—provide a sense of belonging or fellowship

—show an interest in and prayerful concern for the helpee, his helper, and their relationship

—provide practical and tangible help for people in need

—provide opportunity for the person in need to serve others (this is good therapy)

—show a Biblical love to people who don't feel loved, but need it

—provide a meaningful philosophy of life

—support and guide individuals and families in times of crises

—encourage confession of sin and commitment to a sovereign Christ

—give advice and encouragement to the counselor when he faces difficult counseling situations

—guide individuals toward maturity in their relationship to the transcendent Christ

—encourage the helpee as he develops new behavior

—provide a variety of models of maturity and psychological-spiritual stability

—accept sufferers, including former alcoholics, prisoners, mental patients, and others who feel unwelcome in the community as a whole.

OBSTACLES TO HELPING

It doesn't take long for most of us to realize that the body of Christ isn't performing as it should. There are exceptions, of course, but in many places the church is creating problems rather than serving as a therapeutic community. There are at least four reasons for this, all of which must be changed if we want to be really effective people helpers.

Isolation

Several years ago a book appeared with the title *We*,

The Lonely People.[12] The author, Ralph Keyes, observed that most of us want a greater sense of closeness but that we nevertheless spend our lives resisting this closeness. We want to have close, intimate friends who know us, love us, and are available to help in times of need. But we want other things more—things like privacy, mobility, convenience, and the freedom to do our own thing.

Think about how this applies to the church. A lot of us don't want to feel tied to a local body of believers. We want the freedom to move, and we are unwilling to risk getting close to other people within the body (or without) lest one of us move and we face a painful separation. As a result we maintain a detached aloofness—like the kindergartner who wants to play with the other kids but stands on the sidelines, unsure about how to be a member of the group and afraid of being rejected if he tries to join. When and if we do build a good rapport with someone else we resent the intrusion of newcomers—and we realize that existing groups might resent us in a similar way. As a result the body of Christ is often like every other organization in the society. It is composed of people who avoid closeness because they are unwilling to take the risks that come with a greater sense of community. As a body of believers with a common allegiance to Christ and mutually supporting gifts, we ought to be different from every other group in the society—but we aren't. There is something terribly wrong when the church has to sponsor sensitivity groups to build intimacy. If the body is to be a helping community, we need to return to the Biblical pattern of koinonia and dare to get closer to each other.

Insincerity

Centuries ago the prophet Isaiah strongly condemned insincerity (Isa. 1:10-15), and in one of the most stinging speeches of His life Jesus criticized the religious leaders of His day because of their hypocrisy (Matt. 23). They were people who pretended to be pious and devout but in reality were self-centered, dishonest, arrogant phonies. Later, the Apostle Paul told Timothy that hypocrisy would characterize the latter days of the earth's existence. People who claimed to believe one thing would contradict this with their behavior (1 Tim. 4:1-3).

The word "phony" implies something bad, and most of us would like to think that it applies not to us but to someone else—or to another congregation. When students and other people criticize us for being insincere, we ignore it or try to pass it off as the irresponsible prattle of idealistic youth. But it is not easy to feel comfortable when we are being called a hypocrite, and it is difficult to dismiss the penetrating analysis of a man like Keith Miller.

> We train our children to be subtly dishonest almost from the crib. . . . We train our children to *look* happy and successful, to hide their true feelings, their true needs. By the time they are grown, their natural reaction is to put forth immediately the image expected of them in almost any given situation—regardless of how they may honestly feel about that situation.
>
> The result is our churches are filled with people who outwardly look contented and at peace but inwardly are crying out for someone to love them . . . just as they are—confused, frustrated, often frightened, guilty, and often unable to communicate even within their own families. But the *other* people in the church *look* so happy and contented that one seldom has the courage to admit his own deep needs before such a self-sufficient group as the average church meeting appears to be. . . .
>
> Consequently our modern church is filled with many people who look pure, sound pure, and are inwardly sick of themselves, their weaknesses, their frustration, and the lack of reality around them in the church. Our non-Christian friends feel either "that bunch of nice untroubled people would never understand my problems;" or the more perceptive pagans who know us socially or professionally feel that we Christians are either grossly protected and ignorant about the human situation or are out-and-out hypocrites who will not confess the sins and weakness our pagan friends know intuitively to be universal.[13]

Miller goes on to suggest a way out of this hypocrisy. A

new style of life is needed in the church, he suggests, one that "begins with an honesty which really believes that all of us have sinned and fallen short of the glory of God."[14] We need to be honest with ourselves, considering our own strengths and weaknesses. We need to be honest before God, recognizing that He knows all about us anyhow but expects us to confess our sins to Him (1 John 1:9) and to seek His help in coping with inner conflicts. Only then are we secure enough to be honest with each other, sharing our problems and finding compassion from others (Prov. 28:13).

This may sound easier than it really is. It takes courage to share our feelings honestly, to confess our sins and to be open about our burdens. People react to this in several ways. Some will be most uncomfortable and will either withdraw or try to change the subject, while others will be critical. Most people, however, will welcome the openness, and, after their initial surprise and discomfort they might even try opening up a little themselves.

Inactivity

Writers sometimes like to picture the church as being like a big football game where a few men, desperately in need of rest, entertain and are watched by thousands of spectators who are desperately in need of exercise. For some reason we have come to view the church as a place where a few leaders do all the work and most of the members are passive. Little wonder there is no maturing! Inactive organisms always dry up and become progressively weaker.

There are reasons for this deadness in the church. Some people are too busy with other things, some are lazy, and perhaps many have never stopped to realize that the pastor's job is not to do everything. He should, instead, be a "player coach"[15] who helps people to discover their gifts and encourages them to get busy in developing these gifts. The result would be a church on fire, a church characterized by power, love, discipline, and bold evangelism (2 Tim. 1:6-8). This does not mean that the pastor stops preaching. I agree with Helmut Thielicke that "wherever we find, even in this day, a vital, living congregation we find at its center vital preaching."[16] But we also find obedient, lively, active members of the body.

Perhaps one of the reasons for our inactivity, especially as people helpers, is that we don't really know what to do. We have so drawn apart from each other that we feel awkward and embarrassed when someone needs help. Recently one of our neighbors died rather suddenly, and within half an hour my wife had a cake in the oven to take to the family. "You can't do that," I protested. "We don't even know these people and they'll think it strange for us to approach them in this way." Regretfully, my point was taken, we ate the cake ourselves, and we paid a brief visit to the funeral home to sign the visitor's book. But my wife had the better idea—we need to be more open to giving practical help in times of need, even when we "don't know the people."

Human problems seem to come in two varieties—the socially acceptable and the taboo. Socially acceptable troubles include a death in the family, serious illness, a fire or tornado, or the birth of a deformed child. They may be uncomfortable and a little uncertain about what to do, but people gather around at such times bringing food, sympathy, offers of shelter, and other practical help.

When a family faces a taboo problem, things are different. Divorce in the family, a son in jail, an illegitimate teenage pregnancy, alcoholism—people in these situations desperately need help but often don't get it. It is true that in some of these situations sin may be involved, but nowhere in Scripture do we read that sinners or their families should be denied help. Indeed, the opposite is true, yet many times we prefer to say nothing, do nothing, and hope that the embarrassing problem will go away. This may be the most deplorable type of inactivity because it denies help to those who are struggling alone and most in need of others.

Interpersonal Humanism

Within recent years a new movement has been developing within the evangelical church. Known as interpersonal or relational theology, this movement puts a great emphasis on the individual with his needs or problems and on interpersonal relationships between people. It is a movement which arose because people were discovering that knowing all the right theology and Bible verses didn't prevent the breakup of Christian families, drug abuse, or premarital sex among teenagers from Christian homes and churches, as well as caustic or spiteful church business meetings and a host of other problems. Many Christians began to realize that just "believing" the right things is no guarantee that our lives will be straightened out or that interpersonal relations between members of the body will be loving and supportive.

Perhaps the emphasis on interpersonal theology was stimulated by the increasing popularity of psychiatry and psychology. Undoubtedly the widespread interest in church renewal also had some effect. But probably the writings of Bruce Larson and Keith Miller have done more than anything else to wake us up to the need for better interpersonal relations in the church. With its emphasis on such things as sharing, honesty, small group discussion, problem-centered meetings, and sermons dealing with topics like marriage relationships and interpersonal relations, this approach to theology has had a far-reaching, healthy influence on the church. At last we are beginning to know and understand each other and to work harder at getting along together.

With anything fresh and new, however, there is always the danger of an overreaction, and in the case of interpersonal theology the danger is that of degenerating into an interpersonal *humanism*, whereby we become so engrossed in psychological concerns, "helping one another," and "being honest" that we lose sight of the Biblical basis for our fellowship. In some churches and small groups, overzealous adherents of interpersonal theology put so much emphasis on personal experience, building interpersonal relations, and knowing ourselves that the Scriptures are virtually ignored or forgotten. Soon these groups overlook the basis for our Christian fellowship (our oneness as committed disciples of Jesus Christ). The mandate to be building disciples, with all the costs involved, is neglected. Biblical teachings about sin, the need for confession and commitment, the power of the Holy Spirit, and the nature of the body of Christ are de-emphasized and sometimes eventually forgotten. In the end, the dead theology of the past is replaced by an experience-centered form of present-day humanism.

Very few people enjoy dead churches. We should welcome the fresh breezes that interpersonal theology brings while at the same time maintaining the Scriptural foundations on which Christianity is built. Sermons and church programs must be built on the Bible, but these same sermons and programs must show that Christianity is relevant, practical, and able to deal with the problems and concerns in individual lives.

In my classes I tell students that as they speak, hearers should be drawn to Christ and should be able to give a good answer to the question "So what?" If our church programs involve talking to ourselves about obtuse theological issues, then we are not building up the body of Christ any more than does a humanistic sensitivity group. But if we are pointing people to Christ and showing them how Biblical Christianity really makes a difference in their lives, homes, and relationships with others, then the body begins to grow as it should and everyone is helped.

THE HELPING BODY

From the time of its beginning the body of Christ, the church, has been a helping community. There has been isolation, insincerity, inactivity, backbiting, non-cooperation, dishonesty, rigidity, and a host of other pagan

practices in the church, but there has also been a small
"company of the committed" who have built their local
churches on New Testament principles. These are the con-
gregations which most likely have demonstrated the four
helping actions of the church: healing, sustaining, guiding,
and mending broken interpersonal relationships.[17]

To be a true helping community as it was meant to be,
the church must first return to the Biblical pattern of *every*
member committing his or her life to Christ, developing individual spiritual gifts (including the gift of counseling),
and actively using these to minister to others as we move
toward Christian maturity. Individuals who work at this on
their own can and often do help people. But the body working as a unit is much more desirable and effective in really
helping others.

Second, we must remember that the body as a whole
can take specific actions to meet human needs. The church
can encourage and pray for helpers and helpees, can give
tangible help to those in need (even to those with so-called
taboo problems), can provide a stable and accepting community for members and visitors, and can support the
repentant or cured individual who is making his or her way
back into society. By doing this the body of Christ performs
both therapeutic and preventive helping. This is an effective kind of help because it is peer helping, it is mutual
helping, and it is centered around Jesus Christ, the Head of
the body.

10

HOW TO HELP YOURSELF

Recently I was sitting in a restaurant where, to put it mildly, the service was less than efficient. After a long wait for our coffee, I caught the waiter's attention and asked (politely, I thought) if he could fill my cup. Somewhat curtly he replied, "I'll get to you soon, sir! Can't you see that I have people to wait on?"

A friend who was sitting at the table made a poignant reply: "Hey," he exclaimed, "I'm a people too!"

Perhaps you have thought about this while reading the previous pages. Until now we have talked mostly about how we can help others, but we need to remember that the helper is "a people too," and that sometimes the helper needs to be able to help himself.

There is debate among professional counselors about whether or not we can really help ourselves, especially with psychological problems. Some psychoanalysts believe that self-insight and change *might* come after hundreds of hours of counseling, but that this isn't always a certainty. In contrast, other authors have argued that

> ... it *can* be done. With or without prior psychological sophistication, an individual can read or hear about a new idea, can forcefully set about applying it to his own thought and action, and can carve amazingly constructive changes in his own psyche. Not everyone, of course, can or will do this. And few of those who, theoretically, are able to do so, actually ever will. But some can; and some will. . . . Let us, then, not denigrate self-analysis. . . ."[1]

It is not easy to really help ourselves, and at times it isn't even possible, but there are some practical things we can do for a start.

BE A DISCIPLE

When God created mankind, He placed us in a superb environment and clearly intended that human beings should have a close and intimate relationship with their Creator. Unwilling to make us robots, God gave us a will, and with it the freedom to turn against Him. This, of course, is what happened, first in the Garden of Eden and later in the lives of Adam and Eve's descendants.

The Bible uses an unpopular word to describe human rebellion. It is called sin, and it is part of every one of us (Rom. 3:10-12, 23). Sin cuts us off from God, but it does even more than this—it lies at the root of all our problems. Thus, if we are to help people, including ourselves, we must sooner or later face the basic fact of sin. We must first confess our sin and, through prayer, invite Jesus Christ to become Lord of our lives (1 John 1:9; Rom. 10:9). In doing so we are assured of eternal life in heaven and a full, abundant life here on earth (John 3:16; 10:10).

The Bible says nothing about salvation by good works, baptism, church membership, or anything else. Salvation is a gift from God which we can accept, reject or ignore—but never earn (Eph. 2:8, 9; Rom. 6:23).

When a person makes this commitment to Jesus Christ, his or her immediate problems *may* disappear suddenly—but they may also get worse. Yet in the midst of our problems we have peace with God (Rom. 5:1) and a new source of power for coping with life and maintaining mental stability (2 Tim. 1:7). To become a disciple of Jesus Christ is an important part of people helping because it commits our problems to an almighty and wise God who is touched by our difficulties and willing to do something about them (1 Pet. 5:7).

I have a colleague who says at times to counselees, "I don't know what to do about your problem, but I have a

Friend who does!" This is an encouraging truth, especially in times of stress. This divine Friend can help both helpers and helpees.

WALK IN THE SPIRIT

There are a lot of people who commit their lives to Christ but just don't seem to grow spiritually. They stay "babes in Christ" throughout their lives, and because of this immaturity they have trouble understanding the Bible, getting along with people, and dealing with such inner attitudes as jealousy or an exploding temper (1 Cor. 3:1-3). To grow as Christians we need to be imitators of Christ.

Ephesians 5 tells what this means. To be an imitator of Christ means that our life-style is to be characterized by love (Eph. 5:2), moral purity (vv. 3-7), behavior which is pleasing to God (vv. 8-14), wisdom (vv. 15-17), and "being filled with the Spirit" (v. 18). In Galatians 5:16 Paul calls this "walking in the Spirit," and it is the secret of Christian growth.

The Holy Spirit, of course, is the third Person of the Trinity. Jesus promised that the Holy Spirit would come as a Comforter-Teacher, and the disciples experienced the Spirit's power on the Day of Pentecost (Acts 2). When we commit ourselves to Christ, the Holy Spirit comes to live in our inner being. He never leaves, but He can be "quenched" or put down (1 Cor. 6:19; 1 Thes. 5:19). Christians are not to put Him down, but instead are to "walk in the Spirit" every day. This involves frequently examining ourselves and confessing sin, submitting ourselves completely to God and asking the Holy Spirit to fill us (1 John 1:9; Romans 6:11-13; Luke 11:13).[2] Ephesians 5:18 adds that we should keep on being filled with the Spirit, letting Him control our lives daily. The results may not seem outwardly spectacular, but we soon discover (and so do others) that the fruits of the Spirit are growing in our lives: love, joy, peace, patience, kindness, goodness, faithfulness, gentleness, self-control, purity, etc. (Gal. 5:22-26).

All of this does not come as the result of some self-help formula. It is a personality transformation which comes because we have made the decision to walk in the Spirit and let Him control our lives and emotions.

In Chapter 3 we suggested that thinking, feeling, and actions are all important in the individual's life. What distinguishes Christians who are walking in the Spirit from other people is the center around which their lives revolve. For the nonbeliever it is the self.[3]

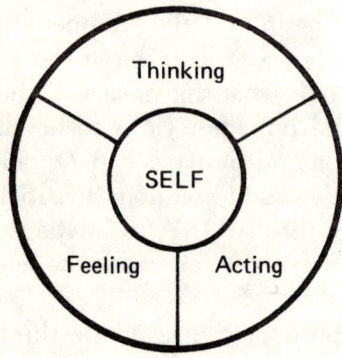

In the nongrowing Christian, Christ has entered his life but has been pushed to the sidelines, so that thinking, feeling, and behavior are still pretty much self-centered and self-directed.

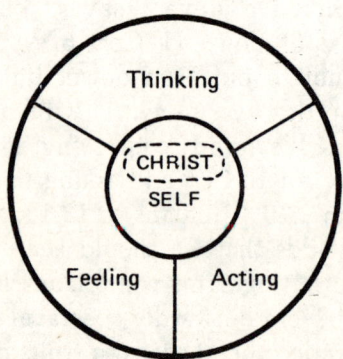

When we walk in the Spirit, however, Christ has come to the center of our lives, and He through the Holy Spirit controls all three parts. Notice that we do not lose our unique personalities so that the self is eliminated. Our self-interests are submitted to Christ, but He works out through the self to influence our thoughts, feelings and actions. When this happens we begin to grow as Christians. This should be a prime goal for disciples and disciplers, including ourselves.

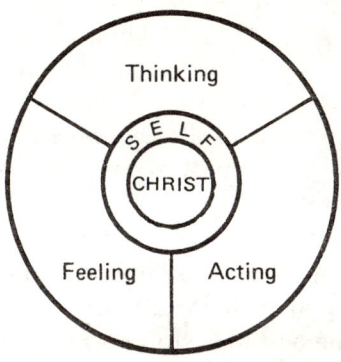

GROW IN MATURITY

The Christian life is not a straitjacket of rules and regulations; it is a life which gives us freedom to grow. But like any growing organism, the Christian grows faster when he or she follows a few health rules.

In Romans 8:29 we read that God wants his followers to be made over into the image of His Son. The goal of our lives is to be like Jesus. Naturally this means that we should get to know Him as intimately as possible. We do this by Bible study and frequent contact with Him through prayer. Every Christian knows this, but so often we find excuses to avoid this intake of spiritual food which is so essential for spiritual growth and development.

In addition to this feeding, exercise is also vital. Have you ever noticed how often the Bible links *what God does for us* with *what we do for others*? The Lord's Prayer is a good example: "Forgive us our debts, as we also have forgiven our debtors. . . . For if you forgive men for their transgressions, your heavenly Father will also forgive you. But if you do not forgive men, then your Father will not forgive your transgressions" (Matt. 6:12-15).

In the Sermon on the Mount the principle is repeated: "Blessed are the merciful, for they shall receive mercy" (Matt. 5:7). "In the way you judge, you will be judged; and by your standard of measure, it shall be measured to you" (Matt. 7:2). In writing to the Philippians, Paul assures his readers that his "God shall supply all your needs . . ." but he has just noted that the Philippians had been very generous in supplying Paul's own needs. James warns that "judgment will be merciless to one who has shown no mercy" (James 2:13).

There appears to be a principle here which might apply to people helpers when we want forgiveness, fair treatment, material things, love, help, attention, or any number of other things. The best place to start receiving is by giving to others. By helping someone else, we grow in Christian maturity, we help ourselves in the process, and our needs are met as we provide for others.

DISCOVER AND DEVELOP SPIRITUAL GIFTS

In the preceding chapter we discussed the fact that every believer has a spiritual gift or gifts. By discovering these gifts and developing them we find our real purpose in life and have the satisfaction of making our unique contribution to the body of Christ.

Although the Bible doesn't give us an exact formula for finding our spiritual gifts, we can be sure that the same God who tells us we have gifts will help us find what they are. We can begin by asking ourselves questions such as the following:[4]

—What spiritual abilities do others see in me?

—What am I most often asked to do—and what am I never asked to do?

—What do I enjoy doing? (God is not a killjoy; He wants us to be happy in the way we serve Him.)

—In what am I most successful? (This may require a little trial and error.)

—Do these successful activities enrich or profit others?—and build up the body of Christ?

Our gifts will soon begin to emerge clearly, but even before we have a complete knowledge of our gifts we can start serving. By trial and error we soon discover those gifts which are given to us by God and are useful for helping the whole body of Christ.

BE A BURDEN SHIFTER

In a thought-provoking little book, J. B. Phillips once argued that "the trouble with many people today is that they have not found a God big enough for modern needs."[5] They have developed a view of God which is too small.

I wish Phillips or somebody like him would write a book to show that for most Christians, our God is not only too small but our burdens are too big. We have a wonderful way of *talking about* divine greatness but ignoring this fact when we face pressures in life. In the Old and New Testaments we are told to cast our burdens on the Lord (Psa. 55:22; 1 Pet. 5:7), and Jesus emphasized this in His Sermon on the Mount and later (Matt. 6:25; 11:28, 29). But Christians are slow to get the message. We either carry all our cares on our own shoulders or we give them to God in prayer and then take them right back.

Paul had this problem. He had a thorn in the flesh which he kept worrying about. One day he got smart, realized that God knew all about his burden, let Him handle the situation, and relaxed (2 Cor. 12:7-10). In contrast, Jacob of the Old Testament tried to run his own life. He engaged in intellectual scheming and even deception to get his way, but when he went to stay with Laban he met someone who was equally crafty. Only as he wrestled with God was Jacob able to submit and hand his whole life over to the Lord.

The North American spirit of independence and rugged individualism gets many of us into a similar bind. When there are financial difficulties, problems in dealing with a wayward child, the need to find a new place to live, or the desire to expand a ministry, we start scheming to make it all happen. Sometimes we succeed and sometimes we fail, but often we carry a burden which shouldn't be ours to bear. This is not a plea for inactivity and a lack of foresight; it is a reminder that our sovereign God knows all about our lives. We need to develop the practice of casting our burdens on Him and trusting Him to work out solutions instead of trying to do everything ourselves. This is an important step in self-help: to "cease striving" and know that He is the exalted God (Psa. 46:10).

TAKE A LOOK AT YOURSELF

In the medical world, diagnosis of a problem usually precedes treatment, and the same is true in helping ourselves (and others). If we can find out what's wrong and what needs to be changed, we are well on the way to doing something about our problem.

Of course this is a lot easier said than done. It is difficult to examine our own lives with much objectivity, and even after we get some idea of what to do, change is not always easy. Nevertheless, this self-examination is important in self-help, and it can take place on three levels.

In the Light of Scripture

First, we can look at ourselves in the light of Scripture. Psalm 119 begins with some advice in this area:
How blessed are those whose way is blameless,
Who walk in the law of the Lord. . . .
How can a young man keep his way pure?

By keeping it according to Thy Word. (Psa. 119:1, 9)

In our daily reading of the Bible we need to be testing our behavior, attitudes, thinking, and feeling against the divine Word of God. God knows our inner psychic problems and struggles better than we do. He can help us to know ourselves better, and His Holy Spirit will assist us as we change (Psa. 139). Before reading the Bible, we should ask God to teach us the specific things we need to know about ourselves and about God Himself.

As You See Yourself

Second, we can look at ourselves in terms of our own perceived strengths and weaknesses. In my seminary course in counseling, each student is required to write an autobiography which includes a listing of his strengths and weaknesses, his goals and life priorities, and his present problems and plans for changing his life-style to make things better. Sometimes this is a difficult assignment, but almost always it is a valuable exercise because it forces each student to take an honest look at himself.

As Others See You

But this autobiography is even more helpful if the student can share it with somebody else. This brings us to the third way of knowing ourselves: sharing with another person. According to psychologist Sidney Jourard, "When a man does not acknowledge to himself who, what, and how he is, he is out of touch with reality, and he will sicken . . . . And it seems to be another fact that no man can come to know himself except as an outcome of disclosing himself to another person."[6] Jourard argues further that a healthy personality is the one who takes the risk of making himself known to at least one other significant human being. Maladjusted people, on the other hand, have not revealed themselves to others and as a result don't know themselves. Such an individual

> struggles actively to avoid becoming known by another
> human being. He works at it ceaselessly, twenty-four
> hours daily, and it is work! In the effort to avoid becom-
> ing known, a person provides for himself a cancerous kind
> of stress which is subtle and unrecognized, but none-
> theless effective in producing not only the assorted
> patterns of unhealthy personality which psychiatry talks
> about, but also the wide array of physical ills that have
> come to be recognized as the province of psychosomatic
> medicine.[7]

In short, in order to look at ourselves accurately we must
be honest before God, with ourselves, and with other
people. This is difficult and risky, but it can be very helpful
for each of us.

LEARN TO ACCEPT YOURSELF

Every one of us has a self-concept, a picture of who we
are and what we are like. If you think "I'm a good
Christian," "I'm a poor housekeeper," "I'm too fat," or
"I'm God's gift to women," these are all part of your self-
concept or self-image.

The best way to get a clear picture of this is to write a
list of adjectives which describe you. The list may include
your physical features (good-looking, balding, big nose,
etc.), your personality characteristics (friendly, impatient,
etc.), your abilities and beliefs ("I am a woman who
believes in God"), your moral values ("I am a person who is
opposed to abortion"), and the various roles that you fulfill
(such as husband, father, son, deacon, businessman, Boy
Scout leader, etc.). In looking over the list you will find that
some of the things listed are desirable (e.g., being friendly)
while others are not (e.g., being lazy). Some parts of your
self-image you hold pretty firmly, while other parts you
aren't so sure about. This list will probably reflect only your
conscious self-image, but there may be some unconscious
characteristics too.

This self-image is important because it determines a lot
of our behavior. If a person sees himself as being a capable

businessman, he will operate much differently than the person who believes he has no business sense. Others may disagree with our self-analysis, but most often we behave, think, and even feel in accordance with this self-concept which has built up over years of learning.

Many Christians have developed the attitude that committed believers should have a poor self-image, that it is a mark of spiritual maturity for the Christian to be always putting himself down. Because of this attitude many of our lives are miserable and we go around boasting about how no-good we are.

We need to recognize that while we were and are sinners, absolutely incapable of bringing about our own salvation, we are also human beings created in the image of God. In fact God valued us so much that He sent His Son to pay the penalty for our sin through His own death. We are not forced to submit our lives to this Christ—God allows us to have some free choice—but when we do, we become new creatures. We are filled with the Holy Spirit, given special spiritual gifts, and accorded the privilege of serving the sovereign God of the universe. God now considers us His own sons and daughters (Rom. 8:15; Gal. 4:4-7; Eph. 5:1), whom He knows and cares for personally. It is true, of course, that none of this came because we are worthy of special treatment. It came solely because of the goodness of God. But this should change our self-image drastically. We are somebody important, a child of the King—because of what He has done. Therefore we can have a positive self-concept. We don't deny our abilities or successes in life. We accept them as coming from God, acknowledge them with gratitude, praise Him for them, and develop a positive self-image based on what God has done in our lives.

DO SOMETHING POSITIVE

Sometimes activity is the best therapy. Alcoholics Anonymous discovered this many years ago and developed a successful rehabilitation program, in which people with a drinking problem help each other.

Many of us are probably guilty of what has been called the gold rush syndrome.[8] In gold-rush days the prospector didn't dare stop to help another man who might be having trouble. To do so was to lose time, and then someone else, maybe even the man he stopped to help, might beat him out for the best claim. The result was a highly individualized, self-centered, private existence. Like the men who passed by the wounded traveler before the Good Samaritan came along, we hurry on through life, engrossed in our own little worlds and perhaps bearing our own burdens. We push toward our own goals and fail to realize that to help another person has great therapeutic value for ourselves. This isn't the only solution to our problems, but when we help somebody else we often get the greatest benefit ourselves.

FIND A COUNSELOR

Surely one of the best ways to help ourselves is to find someone who can help us get a better perspective on life and cope with our problems. Many of us are most reluctant to do this. It seems to imply that we are weak, since we cannot solve our own problems. In reality, however, to find a helper and admit our weakness is really a sign of strength (2 Cor. 12:10). It means that we have faced the problem squarely and decided to find another person whose expertise and objectivity can help us—just as we at some time might help him or her.

Receiving help is always difficult. It puts us under obligation to repay. It can make us feel weak or inferior and it contradicts the rugged individualism that we have come to value so highly. In reality we are all weak and in need of each other, but many of us fail to recognize this fact. To get the help we need makes a lot more sense than sitting around feeling sorry for ourselves and struggling (with repeated failures) to get on top of a situation which we may not fully understand or control. One of the factors which makes for growth in maturity is to accept the help and ministry of other Christians and counselors.[9]

REMEMBER OUR GOAL

In all of our helping, whether helping ourself or others, let us never lose sight of our goal. The Great Commission instructs, indeed commands, every Christian to be witnessing and making disciples. Given power by Christ, we are to be His instruments in changing lives.

The change starts with us as individuals. Are we really followers of Christ? Are we growing as disciples? Are we reaching others with the message of the gospel? Are we reaching out to assist others in the body of Christ as they grow to Christian maturity? Are we, like Paul, contributing to the training of others (including our family members) so that they in turn can be disciples and disciplers? If the answer to any of these questions is no, then we need to make changes in our own lives. If we can answer yes, we are already people helpers, whether we realize it or not.

Part Two

THE HERITAGE OF
PEOPLE HELPING

11
COUNSELING PAST AND PRESENT

The helping of other people has been with us for centuries. The Old Testament is filled with examples of godly men and women who were used by the Holy Spirit to encourage, guide, support, confront, advise, and in other ways help those in need. Jesus was described as a "Wonderful Counselor," and His followers were appointed not only to preach but to deal with the spiritual and psychological needs of individuals (Matt. 10:7, 8). The New Testament epistles give great insight into the counseling techniques of their inspired writers, and later, throughout the Christian era, church leaders have engaged in the four best-known pastoral counseling functions: healing, sustaining, guiding, and reconciling.[1]

Major responsibility for counseling probably rested at one time with theologians, but for some reason counseling shifted from theology into medicine and later into such fields as psychiatry, psychology, and social work. By the first half of this century, counseling had become more and more identified as a specialized discipline. It became set apart from the church, assumed to be out of the range of the pastor's skill and strictly off-limits for untrained laymen.

THE RISE OF PROFESSIONAL COUNSELING

Undoubtedly the influential Dr. Freud (who sometimes gets more blame than he deserves) was partially responsible for the professionalization of counseling. Freud believed that psychotherapy was as skillful a task as surgery and thus not something to be attempted by the untrained. Unlike some of his followers, Freud believed that laymen could be counselors, but that these had to be highly skilled laymen. Pastors were eligible to take this training but, according to Freud and the psychology which he founded, religious people invariably had neurotic hangups which could interfere with their counseling effectiveness.[2] He assumed that to be truly effective a counselor must first undergo hundreds of hours of counseling himself in order to get insights into his own behavior and neuroses.

Pastors, of course, continued to counsel in spite of these psychiatric analyses, and so did laymen. But the non-professional often felt inadequate as a counselor, unsure what to do, and unconvinced that he really could help people with their problems.

In the 1950's and 1960's things began to change. A U.S. government-sponsored report urged upon us the need for training laymen to counsel, and the United States Congress began to allocate money for this purpose. At this time I was in graduate school and can still remember the tone of disbelief in the voice of one of my professors, who informed us that as professionals we were going to have to make room for lay counselors whether we liked the idea or not, and whether or not we thought this was good for the emotionally disturbed people of America.

At about this same time some disturbing reports began to appear, suggesting that while laymen may be poor counselors, professionals might not be much better and in many cases were worse. Hans Eysenck, a controversial British psychologist, published the results of some research which seriously challenged the effectiveness of psychotherapy.[3] Eysenck's work was strongly criticized, but other researchers took up the task and concluded that perhaps two-thirds of all therapists are either ineffective or harmful,[4] including some of the most highly paid professionals. This was hardly a rousing cheer in favor of professional counseling, and the professional image was tarnished still further when the much-acclaimed work of psychologist Robert Carkhuff demonstrated that lay persons with very little training could be very effective in bringing about change in the lives of people with psychological problems.[5]

THE RISE OF PASTORAL COUNSELING

During all this time pastors and laymen were continuing to counsel and help people in a variety of ways. Most of them, I suspect, were oblivious of the debate that was occurring in the professions, and many were encouraged by the increasing influence of something known as the pastoral counseling movement. Begun in the 1920's by a group of pastors and physicians, this movement made great progress, especially in the more liberal theological seminaries.

The best-known "founding father" of the pastoral counseling movement was probably Anton T. Boisen, a minister and writer who, during the first sixty years of his long life, experienced a number of psychotic breakdowns, three of which led to hospitalization in mental institutions. As a result of these experiences, Boisen concluded that the church was neglecting the field of mental health, and he became concerned with the need for training seminary students to work with the mentally ill. Beginning with only a few students, Boisen began a loosely organized training program for seminarians at Worcester State Hospital in Massachusetts.

From this simple beginning, "Clinical Pastoral Education" (CPE) has grown to become a highly organized discipline which provides supervised counseling training for seminarians and pastoral counselors. Much of the CPE work has been admirable: providing standards and guidelines for training pastoral counselors; alerting hospital personnel to the relevance and importance of pastoral involvement in treating the physically and mentally ill; investigating ways in which theology and the psychological sciences can be related; showing the importance of counseling training to seminary education; demonstrating that the personal and spiritual development of the seminarian is at least as important as his intellectual training for the ministry.[6]

In the 1930's and 1940's, when numerous seminaries were adding clinical pastoral training to their curricula, theologically conservative schools were reacting with skepticism—a skepticism which remains to the present. From its beginning CPE appeared to be a theologically liberal movement, and this fact, coupled with a general distrust of psychology, undoubtedly caused evangelicals to stay apart from the CPE mainstream. While in no way endorsing CPE theology, Christian psychologists Clyde Narramore and Henry Brandt demonstrated that a Biblical approach to counseling was possible, and some evangelicals began to see the relevance of psychology to theological education. Now most conservative seminaries and Bible schools have courses in pastoral counseling, and some of these institutions even have highly developed departments of pastoral psychology and counseling. Evangelical contact with the CPE movement tends to remain minimal, however, and there are still no clearly delineated or widely accepted Biblical approaches to the counseling process.

SECULAR COUNSELING TODAY

In a popular magazine, the writer of a recent article estimated that there are currently over two hundred different systematic approaches to counseling! Each of these approaches has enthusiastic advocates, and together the various systems have produced an estimated ten thousand counseling techniques! Some of these approaches, such as psychoanalysis, client-centered counseling, and rational-emotive therapy, are well-known. Other methods are less visible and have fewer followers. Primal scream therapy, radical therapy, dance therapy and many of the body therapies would fall into this latter category.

Directive Therapies

At the risk of oversimplification, we could group these

various systems into three broad and overlapping categories. First, there are the *directive therapies*. In these approaches the counselor is viewed as an expert who diagnoses and analyzes a problem, sometimes labels or categorizes behavior, decides on solutions for the counselee's problem, and in various ways communicates these solutions to the counselee.

Undoubtedly the best example of this approach is the rational-emotive therapy (RET) of Albert Ellis. Ellis assumes that man is a rational, feeling, acting organism—in that order.[7] In order to help people with their problems, Ellis believes that we should not waste time on feelings and actions. Instead, we must focus on thinking; we must teach people to control their fate by learning to think more rationally. Unlike most other approaches to counseling, RET encourages counselors (rather than counselees) to do most of the talking, to directly challenge the counselee's ideas about himself or his world, and, if necessary, to argue, ridicule, command, or even swear at the counselee in order to change his thinking.[8]

Much more gentle, but no less directive, are the psychoanalytic therapies. Here the focus is on the unconscious. It is assumed that problems often arise because of the influence of inner forces which the counselee neither recognizes nor understands. The counselor's job is to listen as the counselee talks freely or describes his dreams. Eventually the counselor begins to see the unconscious causes for the counselee's behavior, and this information is shared in a carefully planned way.

Very different are the various behavior modification therapies. These approaches usually deny that there is such a thing as an unconscious which underlies and produces symptoms. For the behaviorist there is little emphasis on feelings or thinking. It is assumed instead that symptoms *are* the problem, and that the only effective treatment is for behavior or actions to be changed through the use of techniques derived from the laboratories of psychological researchers. The emphasis here is on changing what people *do* (rather than what they think or feel), sometimes even without the counselee's awareness or desire for treatment. The therapist is supposed to be an expert in analyzing a problem situation and knowing how the counselee's actions can be altered.

Permissive Therapies

Very much opposite from these directive approaches is a group of treatment techniques which might be labeled the nondirective or *permissive therapies*. The counselor here may see himself as an expert in dealing with personal problems, but his task is not to make diagnoses, prescribe solutions, or treat people. Instead, the counselor is a facilitator who stimulates people to solve their own problems and who creates a permissive environment where this problem can be solved and personal growth can occur.

The early client-centered therapy of Carl Rogers is the best-known example of this approach. The therapist seeks to show warmth, understanding, empathy, concern, and "unconditional positive regard" for his "client," who in turn feels free to express his frustrations and feelings. There is no attempt to direct the conversation, interpret what is going on, give advice, or render blame. The counselor listens as the counselee-client talks, summarizes what has been said, and tries to identify what the client is feeling. It is assumed that the client will eventually get insight into his own behavior and will take steps to change.

Within recent years, Rogers has moved more and more into the use of group therapy, in which clients help each other with problems. While they differ widely in their assumptions and goals, the Gestalt therapy of Perls, the various encounter therapies, the experiential psychotherapy of Gendlin, and some of the existential therapies also see value in group interaction. In addition, each of these methods focuses on the innate potential of man, emphasizes human experience and feelings, and assumes that individual human beings are able to work out their own problems when given the appropriate permissive therapeutic conditions.[9]

Interactional Therapies

At some point between the directive and permissive approaches to counseling are what might be called the *interactional therapies*. This term describes counseling in which the counselor and counselee interact together more or less as equals. A Swiss physician named Paul DuBois used this approach around the turn of the century. DuBois reportedly "held conversations with his patients and taught them a philosophy of life whereby they substituted in their minds thoughts of health for their customary preoccupations with. . .disease. . . . He insisted that the physician treat the patient as a friend, not merely as an interesting case."[10]

DuBois has been described as the "most direct spiritual ancestor" of William Glasser, whose reality therapy is, in essence, a team effort between counselor and counselee. The reality therapist does not deny feelings or behavior, but he encourages the counselee to focus on present reality and to work out plans for the future which will help him feel loved, able to love, and more worthwhile as a human being.

These three broad approaches to counseling might be summarized by the following diagram:[11]

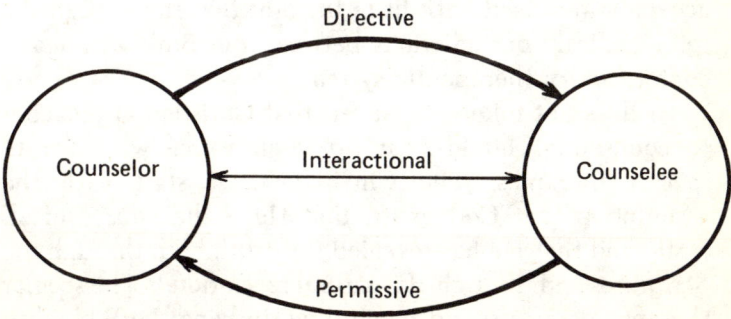

In any counseling situation there are at least two persons involved—the counselor and the counselee. These two people are sometimes referred to by different terms (therapist-patient, helper-helpee, facilitator-client, etc.), and often there is more than one counselee (as in group therapy) or counselor (as in team counseling).

The relationship between these participants is either *directive* (where most of the action moves from the counselor to the counselee), *permissive* (where the counselor is a facilitator of action on the part of the counselee), or *interactional* (where there is more or less a team effort between equals). The dotted line in the center of the diagram is a continuum on which the various therapies might be placed. Some therapies are at one of the extremes, while others are closer to the middle. Some, such as the eclectic theories, would cover a broad part of the continuum, while others are more narrow in their perspective.

CHRISTIAN APPROACHES TO COUNSELING

In his controversial but thought-provoking book *Competent to Counsel*, Jay Adams has charged that much of what we call Christian counseling today involves little more than taking these secular approaches and sprinkling them with a few Bible verses.[12] I suspect that Dr. Adams would agree that for many Christian counselors there hasn't even been a sprinkling! Secular approaches have been accepted and used with little thought that there might be some radical contradictions between the Bible and many contemporary therapeutic systems.

It does not follow, however, that Christian approaches to counseling should bear no resemblance whatever to secular therapies. The Christian must start with the assumption that God exists, that He is the Source of all truth, and that He has revealed this truth both through the Scriptures and through His natural revelation.[13] The secular therapist doesn't spend much time studying the Bible, but at least he is a scientist who studies God's natural revelation. It is not surprising, therefore, that in his study the nonbeliever has found some useful conclusions about human behavior and has stumbled upon some counseling techniques that are both effective and consistent with God's special revelation as found in the Scriptures. When Christians develop approaches to counseling, it should not be surprising that some of their techniques will parallel the secular at least in some ways.

Nouthetic Counseling

Consider, for example, the "nouthetic" counseling of Dr. Adams (from *noutheteo*, the Greek word for admonishing). This is a *directive approach* which is in many respects similar to the rational-emotive therapy of Ellis. Although he has been criticized for many of his conclusions, Adams nevertheless has attempted to build a counseling system which begins with and is built on Scripture. Few others have been courageous or creative enough to attempt such a task.

Adams' approach has been accepted without question by many Christians, perhaps because it gives simple answers, criticizes non-Christian therapies which ignore the Bible, emphasizes the importance of sin, assumes that a seminary education is all one needs for competent counseling, permits the counselor to be directive and authoritarian, and removes responsibility from the counselor by permitting him to cast responsibility for recovery on the counselee. Undoubtedly many Christians are impressed with Dr. Adams' attempts to support his approach Biblically, and it may be that nouthetic counseling has attracted followers because there is no alternative system which is as clearly Biblical.

In the beginning of his book, Adams states that his method is presuppositional. "I avowedly accept the inerrant Bible as the Standard of all faith and practice," he writes. "The Scriptures, therefore, are the basis, and contain the criteria by which I have sought to make every judgment."[14] In a footnote he adds another very important guideline which some of the current popular speakers in psychology might do well to heed. "Case material is used as supporting evidence but only illustratively. Such materials must not be thought to confirm or verify Biblical positions (God's Word does not need human support); I have used it rather to illustrate, concretize and clarify."[15] Adams then goes on to request that anyone who criticizes his work should do so "in a Biblical manner." He is not interested in neutral, objective, empirical data or in debate which arises from non-Christian suppositions.[16]

Adams has the right to list these stipulations, but in so doing he almost puts his system beyond criticism. "I can't accept your criticism unless you accept my assumptions," he says in essence, but it is difficult to find anything to criticize if one accepts his assumptions.

One can, however, fault Adams for his epistemology (view of the source of knowledge) and for his selective hermeneutics (interpretation of Scripture). In terms of epistemology, Adams accepts the authority of the Scriptures but makes the debatable assumption that God has revealed all that we need know about counseling within the pages of the Bible. Certainly God's written revelation is clearer than that which is nonwritten, and the Bible must be accepted as an authority because it is inerrant and the divine Word of God. It does not follow, however, that God reveals all truth about man or about His universe within the pages of Scripture. Medicine, physics, chemistry, and a host of other academic disciplines have discovered truths about God's world which are consistent with, but not *written* in, the pages of the Bible. Why then should we assume that secular psychology and psychiatry are not able to uncover any truth? Certainly the findings of these and other sciences must be tested against the written Word of God, but to dismiss psychology, as Adams has, may be more an evidence of personal prejudice than of Biblical exegesis or rational analysis. As counselors, might it not be better to examine God's special and natural revelation and find in both of these an instructive and practical insight into counseling? Adams himself has done this. He advocates the use of role play, Christian psychological testing, team counseling, and sometimes a Skinnerian form of conditioning,[17] none of which is found in the Bible but all of which can be consistent with Biblical revelation.

As presented in its written form, Dr. Adams' "nouthetic" or admonishment counseling is a directive approach which has little place for encouragement, supportive counseling, or the reassurance and assistance that comes from being in the body of believers. Confrontation is emphasized; listening, compassion, and love are de-emphasized, even though the latter are important Scriptural concepts.

This brings us to Adams' interpretation of Scripture. In an attempt to discredit psychology and build a system which is consistent with the Bible, Adams sometimes appears to be forcing the Scriptures into his own system. Consider, for example, the assumption that behavior determines feelings, and never vice versa. It is true, of course, that good living can produce good feelings and that sinful behavior can create feelings of depression or other problems. But Psalm 34:12, 13; 1 Peter 3; Ephesians 2:10; 4:19; and 1 Timothy 4:2, the passages which Adams cites, can hardly give support to the conclusion that feelings always stem from behavior. One might think of the Pharisees in Jesus' day, whose behavior was morally upright but whose attitudes, emotional reactions, and motives were clearly impure. "Nouthetic counselors," Adams writes, "spend less time finding out how people feel. They are more interested in discovering how clients behave."[18] As we have seen in previous chapters, however, the Scriptures give importance to feelings and thoughts as well as behavior.

We have spent several paragraphs commenting on the work of Dr. Adams because his system is probably the best-known among evangelicals. It also expresses an assumption underlying much of the counseling done by pastors and others who are theologically conservative: that the role of the Christian counselor is to preach in the counseling room. There is a suspicion of any other kind of approach.

Permissive Approaches

The nondirective or more *permissive approaches* to Christian counseling have been advocated most clearly by the early writers in the pastoral counseling movement. Although this is becoming less and less typical of Clinical Pastoral Education today, there was much emphasis on Rogerian techniques during the post-World War Two years. Such an approach was consistent with a liberal theology, which deemphasized original sin and the authority of Scripture, stressed the innate potential of man, and emphasized the individual's ability to solve his own problems. Because of the nonbiblical assumptions on which this approach is built, few evangelicals have accepted it wholeheartedly, although many would agree with Clinebell's observation that the

> . . . profound influence which the client-centered method has had on the development of contemporary pastoral counseling has been . . . helping to rescue it from a legacy of overdirectiveness. It was (and is) particularly needed by *clergymen* to alert us to the twin professional hazards of facile verbalizing and playing god in the lives of counselees. It has demonstrated convincingly the crucial importance in all counseling of disciplined listening and responding to feelings. For ministers in authority-centered traditions and for theological students learning counseling, a time exposure to Roger's approach is highly beneficial. A grounding in this philosophy and method is an excellent *starting* point for increasing one's counseling skills. It is not an adequate *stopping* point. It gives one the fundamentals of establishing a therapeutic relationship, but it does not provide guidance in the *varied* methods of utilizing this relationship to help troubled persons. The Rogerian method provides a firm foundation but not the entire edifice of an adequate approach to counseling. The pastor must stay *person-centered* in his counseling, but this is not synonymous with remaining "client-centered" in methodology.[19]

The Interactional Approach

The pastoral counseling movement now appears to be moving more toward the *interactional approach*. Although he never uses the term, this is the type of counseling proposed many years ago by Paul Tournier, the well-known counselor in Switzerland. Tournier has never taken a course in counseling and maintains that he has no particularly unique approach. Instead, he seeks to engage his counselees in dialogue between two equals. At first there is small talk and nervous laughter, but eventually Tournier tries to build a spiritual communion between counselor and counselee, a trusting person-to-person bond between two human beings. Acceptance, support, mutual sharing, honest confession of sins and personal weaknesses, prayer, passive listening, and directive giving of advice may all be part of counseling.[20]

The interactional approach does not cast the counselor into a role of being the mighty expert or, at the other extreme, of being a catalyst who provides an environment where the counselee can solve his problems. An interactional approach removes the doctor-patient hierarchy and sees the counselor and counselee for what they really are— fellow human beings, created by God in His image and working together at burden-bearing and problem-solving.

In an attempt to further break down the doctor-patient nature of counseling, some have suggested that we should use the term *helper* instead of counselor and substitute the word *helpee* in place of counselee. This has been done in the preceding pages. The helpee is a valuable individual who has a problem, and the helper is God's instrument for teaching and guiding in the life of the helpee. The helpee is an expert in his own problems. He has lived with them, analyzed them, been defeated by them, and tried unsuccessfully to solve them. The helper is also an expert, in counseling techniques and in understanding both the Scriptures and human psychology. The helper is not limited to a few methods. He may comfort, support, question, listen to, encourage, or simply stand alongside the helpee. He recognizes that the Holy Spirit is really the Therapist and that the helper must be a man or woman of God who is a vessel "fit for the Master's use" in molding the life of another and guiding him or her through a counseling situation.

Alternative Approaches

While the interactional approach may be the preferred method of counseling, there will be occasions when either a more direct or a more permissive approach would be of greatest help to the person with a problem. All three have Biblical precedent, and all three are used at times by Christian counselors. The directive approach might be viewed as a prophetic-confrontational approach to counseling, in which the counselor speaks the truth in love and confronts the counselee with his or her failures to take responsibility and live up to Biblical standards. Permissive counseling is more of a priestly-confessional approach, in which the counselee talks about his problems, needs, and sins, and the counselor listens and points the way to forgiveness.[21] "Pastoral-conversational" is a term that could be applied to the interactional approach. Here there is a conversation between counselor and counselee, but there is more. The counselor brings his loving concern and expertise, gently leading the counselee and helping him to grow psychologically and spiritually. The diagram on page 167 could therefore be labeled as follows:

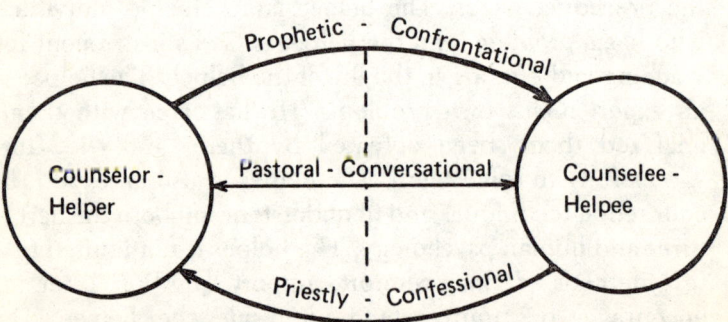

People helping through counseling is a difficult and demanding challenge. The Christian counselor-helper is basically a teacher who assumes the responsibilities and demands that such a position involves.[22] To be a Christian helper is not a task to be taken lightly. It is a committing of oneself to the challenge of being God's instrument for changing another person's life. The responsibilities are great, and so at times are the frustrations, but the rewards in this life and the next make people helping one of the greatest of all challenges which we can share on this earth.

FOOTNOTES

Chapter 1

1. J. D. Pentecost, *Design for Discipleship* (Grand Rapids: Zondervan, 1971), pp. 46, 40, 55.
2. W. A. Henrichsen, *Disciples Are Made—Not Born* (Wheaton, Illinois: Victor Books, 1974), p. 153.
3. Ibid., p. 154.
4. D. Bonhoeffer, *The Cost of Discipleship* (New York: Macmillan, 1937).
5. Pentecost, op. cit., p. 104.
6. G. H. Harvey, S. R. Hoyt, and C. R. Stewart, *You the Discipler: A Strategy for Success* (Wheaton, Illinois: Christian Service Brigade, n.d.), p. 19.
7. G. H. Harvey, personal communication, Georgia State University.

Chapter 2

1. Gary R. Collins, *The Christian Psychology of Paul Tournier* (Grand Rapids: Baker, 1973).
2. See R. R. Carkhuff, *Helping and Human Relations: A Primer for Lay and Professional People, Volume I, Selection and Training* (New York: Holt, Rinehart and Winston, 1969); C. B. Truax, "Therapist Empathy, Genuineness, and Warmth and Patient Therapeutic Outcome," in *Journal of Consulting Psychology*, vol. 30, 1966, pp. 395-401; L. M. Brammer, *The Helping Relationship: Process and Skills* (Englewood Cliffs, New Jersey: Prentice-Hall, 1973).
3. Ibid., Brammer.
4. Ibid.

Chapter 3

1. This diagram is suggested in Anderson and Anderson, *The House Church* (Nashville: Abingdon, 1975), p. 35.
2. Wise King Solomon emphasized the importance of listening before talking in Proverbs 18:13.
3. G. Egan, *The Skilled Helper* (Monterey, California: Brooks/Cole, 1975).

4. L. M. Brammer, *The Helping Relationship: Process and Skills* (Englewood Cliffs, New Jersey: Prentice-Hall, 1973).

5. See, for example, R. E. Coleman, *The Master Plan of Evangelism* (Old Tappan, New Jersey: Fleming H. Revell, 1963); N. A. Henrichsen, *Disciples Are Made—Not Born* (Wheaton, Illinois: Victor Books, 1974). Perhaps the classic book in the field is by A. B. Bruce, *The Training of the Twelve* (Grand Rapids: Kregel, 1971). This book was published originally in 1871. A more recent work, written by Carl Wilson of Worldwide Discipleship Association, is currently under preparation.

6. This is illustrated in 1 Corinthians 3:4-10, where Paul recognizes that discipleship may involve the mutual efforts of a number of believers.

Chapter 4

1. R. R. Carkhuff, "Differential Functioning of Lay and Professional Helpers," in *Journal of Counseling Psychology*, vol. 15, 1968, pp. 117-28.

2. Ibid., p. 117.

3. P. Morris, *Love Therapy* (Wheaton, Illinois: Tyndale House, 1974), pp. 16-17.

4. Carkhuff, op. cit., pp. 119-20.

5. Carkhuff, op. cit., p. 121. See also F. Reissman, "Strategies and Suggestions for Training Nonprofessionals," in *Community Mental Health Journal*, vol. 3, 1967, pp. 103-110; and P. W. Clement, "Parents, Peers and Child Patients Make the Best Therapists," in Gertrude T. Williams and S. Gordon, eds., *Clinical Child Psychology: Current Practices and Future Perspectives* (New York: Behavioral Publications, 1974), pp. 81-97.

6. See, for example, Reissman, op. cit.; R. R. Carkhuff, *Helping and Human Relations: A Primer for Lay and Professional People, Volume I, Selection and Training* (New York: Holt, Rinehart and Winston, 1969); S. J. Danish and Brock, "The Current Status of Training for Paraprofessionals," in *The Personnel and Guidance Journal*, vol. 53, 1974, pp. 299-303; S. J. Danish, *Helping Skills: A Basic Training Program* (New York: Behavioral Publications, 1973); G. Egan, *The Skilled Helper: A Model for Systematic Helping and Interpersonal Relating* (Monterey, California: Brooks/Cole, 1975); J. M. Gottman and S. R. Leiblum, *How to Do Psychotherapy and How to Evaluate It: A Manual for Beginners* (New York: Holt, Rinehart and Winston, 1974); A. E. Ivey, *Microcounseling: Innovations in Interviewing Training* (Springfield, Illinois: C. C. Thomas, 1971); and N. Kagan, "Influencing Human Interaction—Eleven Years of IPR" (unpublished manuscript, Michigan State University, 1975).

7. G. Caplan, *Principles of Preventive Psychiatry* (New York: Basic Books, 1964), p. 49.

8. S. M. Jourard, *The Transparent Self*, rev. ed. (New York: Van Nostrand Reinhold, 1971), p. 5.

9. S. J. Danish, "A Training Program in Helping Skills: An Examination of What, How and If It Works." Paper presented at meetings of the American Psychological Association, New Orleans, Louisiana, 1974.

10. F. Reissman, "The 'Helper' Therapy Principle," in *Social Work*, April 1965, pp. 27-31.

Chapter 5

1. E. H. Erikson, "Identity and the Life Cycle," in *Psychological Issues Monograph*, vol. 1 (New York: International Universities Press, 1959).

2. G. Caplan, *Principles of Preventive Psychiatry* (New York: Basic Books, 1964).

3. G. W. Brockopp, "Crisis Intervention Theory , Process and Practice," in D. Lester and G. W. Brockopp, *Crisis Intervention and Counseling by Telephone* (Springfield, Illinois: Charles C. Thomas, 1973), pp. 89-104; U. Delworth, E. H. Rudow, and J. Taub, *Crisis Center Hotline* (Springfield, Illinois: Charles C. Thomas, 1972).

4. Ibid., Delworth et al., p. 48.

5. T. F. McGee, "Some Basic Considerations in Crisis Intervention," in *Community Mental Health Journal*, vol. 4, 1968, p. 323. Cited in D. K. Switzer, *The Minister as Crisis Counselor* (Nashville: Abingdon, 1974).

6. Brockopp, op. cit., p. 94.

Chapter 6

1. U. Delworth, E. Rudow, and J. Taub, ed., *Crisis Center Hotline* (Springfield, Illinois: Charles C. Thomas, 1972).

2. D. Lester and G. W. Brockopp, *Crisis Intervention and Counseling by Telephone* (Springfield, Illinois: Charles C. Thomas, 1973), p. vii.

3. R. K. McGee and B. Jennings, "Ascending to the 'Lower' Levels: The Case for Nonprofessional Crisis Workers," in Lester and Brockopp, op. cit., pp. 223-237; D. A. Knickerbocker and R. K. McGee, "Clinical Effectiveness of Non Professional and Professional Telephone Workers in a Crisis Intervention Center," in Lester and Brockopp, op. cit., pp. 298-309.

4. S. M. Heilig, "Training in Suicide Prevention," in *Bulletin of Suicidology*, no. 6, pp. 41-44, Spring 1970.

5. Many of the conclusions in this section are adapted from an article by T. Williams and J. Douds, "The Unique Contribution of Telephone Therapy," in Lester and Brockopp, op. cit., pp. 80-89.

6. Ibid., p. 85.

7. See G. W. Brockopp, "The Telephone Call: Conversation or Therapy," in Lester and Brockopp, op. cit., pp. 111-16.

8. C. W. Lamb, "Telephone Therapy: Some Common Errors and Fallacies," in *Voices*, vol. 5, 1969-70, pp. 45-46.

9. P. Tournier, *Escape from Loneliness* (Philadelphia: Westminster, 1962).

10. L. Brammer and L. Shostrom, *Therapeutic Psychology* (Englewood Cliffs, New Jersey: Prentice-Hall, 1968), p. 435.

11. These callers are each discussed in detail in Lester and Brockopp, op. cit., Part III.

12. Ibid., pp. 193-98.

Chapter 7

1. *Prevention of Suicide*. Public Health Papers, No. 35 (Geneva: World Health Organization, 1968), p. 9.

2. *World Health Statistics Report*, vol. 21, no. 6, 1968, pp. 392-94.

3. L. I. Dublin, "Suicide Prevention," in E. S. Shneidman, ed., *On the Nature of Suicide* (San Francisco: Jossey Bass, 1969).

4. Abimelech (Judges 9:53, 54), Samson (Judges 16:28-31), Saul (1 Samuel 31:1-6), Saul's arms-bearer (1 Chronicles 10:4, 5), Ahithophel (2 Samuel 17:23), Zimri (1 Kings 16:18), and Judas Iscariot (Matthew 27:3-5). This list is taken from D. Lumm, *Responding to Suicidal Crisis* (Grand Rapids: Eerdmans, 1974), p. 29.

5. The work of these authors is contained in a number of books and articles. See, for example, E. S. Shneidman and N. L. Farberow, ed., *Clues to Suicide* (New York: McGraw-Hill, 1957); N. L. Farberow and E. S. Shneidman, ed., *The Cry for Help* (New York: McGraw-Hill, 1961); and E. S. Shneidman, N. L. Farberow, and R. E. Litman, *The Psychology of Suicide* (New York: Science House, 1970). Much of the material in this chapter is adapted from this latter work.

6. N. L. Farberow, S. M. Heilig, and R. E. Litman, "Evaluation and Management of Suicidal Persons," in Shneidman, Farberow, and Litman, op. cit., pp. 273-91.

7. E. S. Shneidman, "Preventing Suicide," in *Bulletin of Suicidology*, December 1968, pp. 19-25.

8. E. Robins, J. Gassner, J. Kayes, R. H. Wilkinson, Jr., and G. E. Murphy, "The Communication of Suicide Intent: A Study of 134 Consecutive Cases of Successful (Completed) Suicides," in *American Journal of Psychiatry*, vol. 115, 1959, pp. 724-33.

9. Shneidman, op. cit., p. 25.

10. C. J. Fredrick and L. Lague, *Dealing With the Crisis of Suicide*. Public Affairs Pamphlet No. 406A, New York, 1972.

11. John W. Drakeford, *Farewell to the Lonely Crowd* (Waco, Texas: Word, 1969).

12. O. H. Mowrer, *The Crisis in Psychiatry and Religion* (New York: Van Nostrand, 1961).

13. H. J. Clinebell, Jr., *Mental Health Through Christian Community* (New York: Abingdon, 1965), p. 244. Copyright © Abingdon Press. Quoted with permission.

Chapter 8

1. G. Caplan, *Principles of Preventive Psychiatry*, (New York: Basic Books, 1964).

2. M. Zax and G. A. Specter, *An Introduction to Community Psychology (New York: Wiley, 1974)*.

3. H. J. Clinebell, Jr., *Mental Health Through Christian Community* (Nashville: Abingdon Press, 1965); H. J. Clinebell, Jr., ed., *Community Mental Health: The Role of Church and Temple* (Nashville: Abingdon Press, 1970).

4. *Community Mental Health*, op. cit., p. 11.

Chapter 9

1. M. T. Kelsey, *Healing and Christianity* (New York: Harper & Row, 1973), p. 14.

2. J. A. Knight, "The Therapeutic Opportunity of the Clergyman and the Congregation," in H. J. Clinebell, Jr., ed., *Community Mental Health: The Role of Church and Temple* (Nashville: Abingdon Press, 1970), pp. 84-90.

3. J. S. Beckeven, *Moral Treatment in American Psychiatry* (New York: Springer, 1963).

4. M. Jones, *The Therapeutic Community* (New York: Basic Books, 1953).

5. This paragraph is adapted from R. N. Rapaport, *Community as Doc-*

tor: *New Perspectives on a Therapeutic Community* (Lt Tavistock Publications, 1960).

6. R. Almond, *The Healing Community* (New York: Jason Aronsen, 1974).

7. The discussion in this section is adapted largely from John MacArthur, Jr., *The Church: The Body of Christ* (Grand Rapids: Zondervan, 1973); and Ray C. Stedman, *Body Life* (Glendale, California: Regal, 1972).

8. J. W. Drane, "Fellowship: Our Humpty-Dumpty Approach," in *Christianity Today*, vol. 19, May 9, 1975, pp. 6-8.

9. Stedman, op. cit., p. 107.

10. G. W. Allport, *The Individual and His Religion* (New York: Macmillan, 1950), p. 90.

11. Ibid., p. 93.

12. R. Keyes, *We, The Lonely People* (New York: Harper & Row, 1973).

13. Keith Miller, *The Taste of New Wine* (Waco: Word, 1965), pp. 22, 27.

14. Ibid., p. 27.

15. E. Trueblood, *The Incendiary Fellowship* (New York: Harper & Row, 1967), pp. 43-44.

16. H. Thielicke, *The Trouble with the Church* (New York: Harper & Row, 1965), p. viii.

17. W. A. Clebsch and C. R. Jaekle, *Pastoral Care in Historical Perspective* (Englewood Cliffs, N. J.: Prentice-Hall, 1964).

Chapter 10

1. A. Ellis and R. A. Harper, *A Guide to Rational Living* (Hollywood, California: Wilshire Book Company, 1970), pp. 5-6.

2. These steps are adapted from T. F. LaHaye, "How to Walk in the Spirit," in *Moody Monthly*, September 1973, pp. 38-41, 86-88.

3. This diagram is an adaptation from that published by Anderson and Anderson, *The House Church* (Nashville: Abingdon, 1975), p. 35.

4. Adapted from J. A. Davey, "How to Discover Your Spiritual Gift," in *Christianity Today*, vol. 19, May 9, 1975, pp. 9-11.

5. J. B. Phillips, *Your God Is Too Small* (London: Epworth Press, 1952).

6. S. M. Jourard, *The Transparent Self*, rev. ed. (New York: Van Nostrand Reinhold, 1971), p. 6.

7. Ibid., p. 33.

8. Anderson and Anderson, op. cit., p. 51.

9. R. Stedman, *Body Life* (Glendale, California: Regal Books, 1972), p. 127.

Chapter 11

1. For a discussion of these four functions see W. A. Clebsch and C. R. Jaekle, *Pastoral Care in Historical Perspective* (Englewood Cliffs, New Jersey: Prentice-hall, 1964).

2. S. Freud, *The Future of an Illusion* (Garden City, New York: Doubleday Anchor Books, 1927).

3. H. J. Eysenck, *The Effects of Psychotherapy* (New York: International Science Press, 1966).

4. Allen E. Bergin, "The Evaluation of Therapeutic Outcomes," in A. E. Bergin and S. L. Garfield, ed., *Handbook of Psychotherapy and Behavior Change* (New York: Wiley, 1971,) pp. 217-70.

5. R. R. Carkhuff, "Differential Functioning of Lay and Professional Helpers," in *Journal of Counseling Psychology*, vol. 15, 1968, pp. 117-26. See also R. R. Carkhuff, *Helping and Human Relations: A Primer for Lay and Professional People, Volume I, Selection and Training* (New York: Holt, Rinehart and Winston, 1969).

6. For an excellent overview of the CPE movement see E. E. Thornton, *Professional Education for Ministry: A History of Clinical Pastoral Education* (Nashville: Abingdon, 1970). See also the March 1975 issue of *The Journal of Pastoral Care*, which is a whole issue commemorating the fiftieth anniversary of the founding of CPE.

7. Albert Ellis, *Humanistic Psychotherapy: The Rational-Emotive Approach* (New York: Julian Press, 1973), pp. 70, 77.

8. Albert Ellis, "Rational-Emotive Therapy," in L. Hersher, *Four Psychotherapies* (New York: Appleton-Century-Crofts, 1970), pp. 85-124.

9. For a summary of current approaches to counseling and psychotherapy see C. H. Patterson, *Theories of Counseling and Psychotherapy*, 2nd ed. (New York: Harper & Row, 1973); Raymond Corsini, ed., *Current Psychotherapies* (Itasca, Illinois: Peacock, 1973).

10. Ibid., Corsini, p. 287.

11. Adapted from John Drakeford, *The Awesome Power of the Listening Ear* (Waco, Texas: Word, 1967), p. 30.

12. Jay Adams, *Competent to Counsel* (Grand Rapids: Baker, 1970), p. xxi.

13. For a further elaboration of the Christian counseler's assumptions, see Gary R. Collins, *The Rebuilding of Psychology* (Wheaton: Tyndale House, in press).

14. Adams, op. cit., p. xxi.

15. Ibid.

16. Ibid., p. 269.

17. Ibid., pp. 111, 152, 176, 203.

18. Ibid., p. 93.

19. Howard J. Clinebell, Jr., *Basic Types of Pastoral Counseling* (New York: Abingdon, 1966), pp. 29-30.

20. For a more detailed discussion of Tournier's counseling approach, see Gary R. Collins, *The Christian Psychology of Paul Tournier* (Grand Rapids: Baker, 1973), pp. 118-27.

21. Use of the terms "prophetic" and "priestly" to describe counseling is adapted from an unpublished paper by Professor David E. Carlson, Trinity College, Deerfield, Illinois. The paper, "Jesus' Style of Relating: The Search For a Biblical View of Counseling" was read at the Conference on Research in Mental Health and Religious Behavior, Atlanta, Georgia, January 26, 1976.

22. James 3:1.

INDEX